Be Happy

Barbara Freethy

Also available in the *Be Coloring* series:

Be Free

Be Calm

Be Creative

Be Industrious

To be calm is the highest
achievement of the self.

~ Zen Proverb

Illustrated Contents

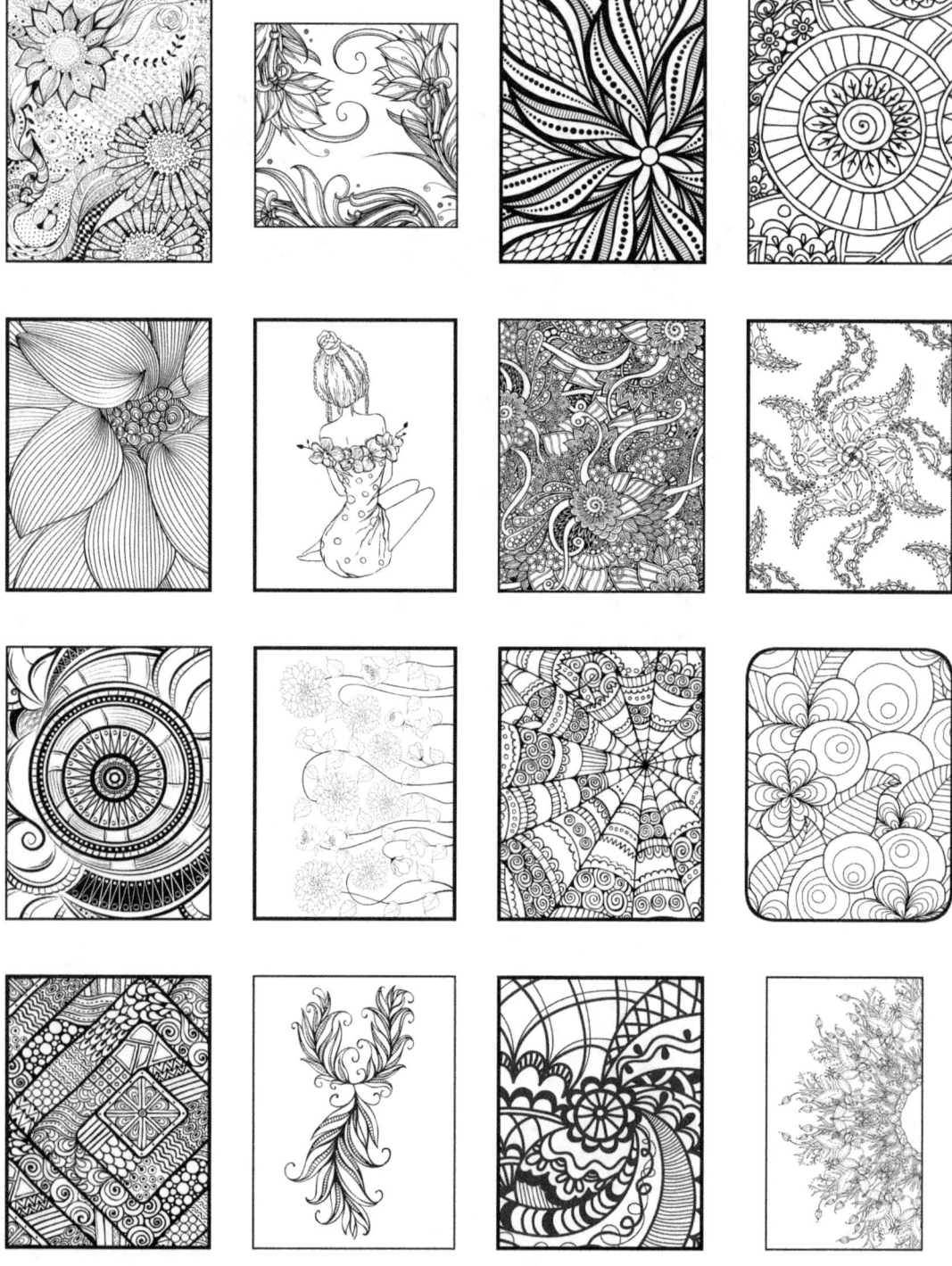

Illustrated Contents

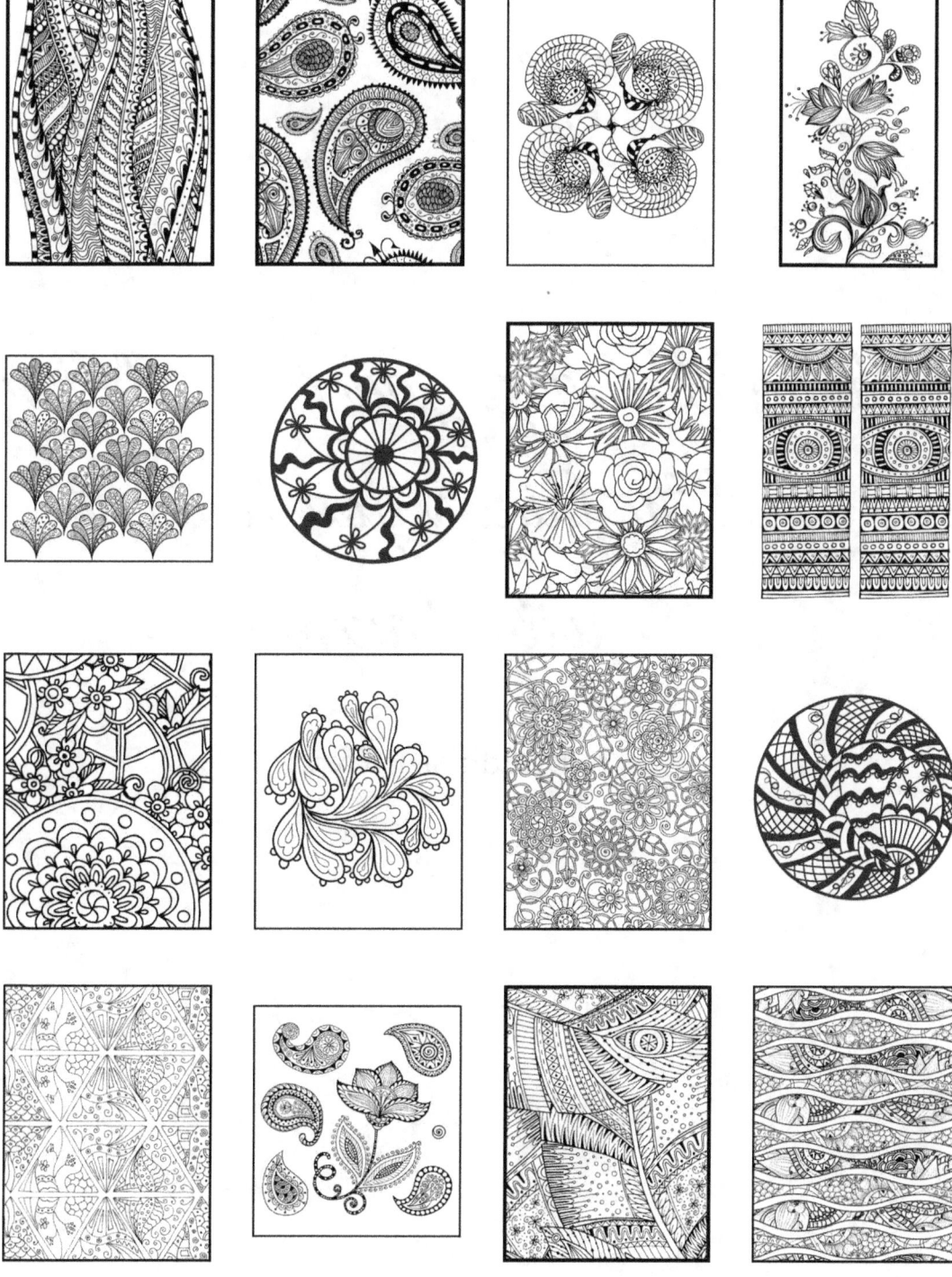

Change the way you look at things, and the things you look at will change.

~ Buddhist Proverb

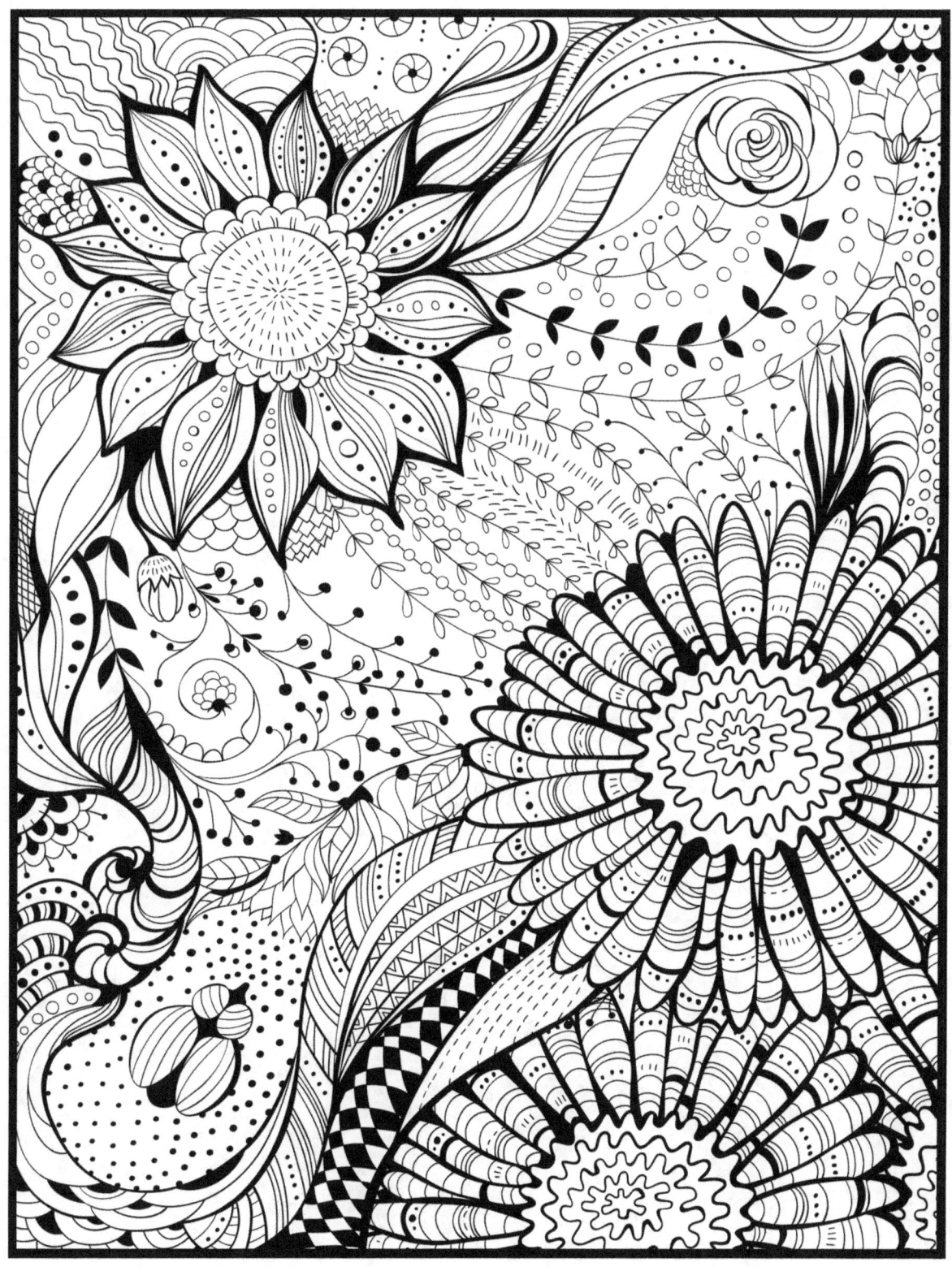

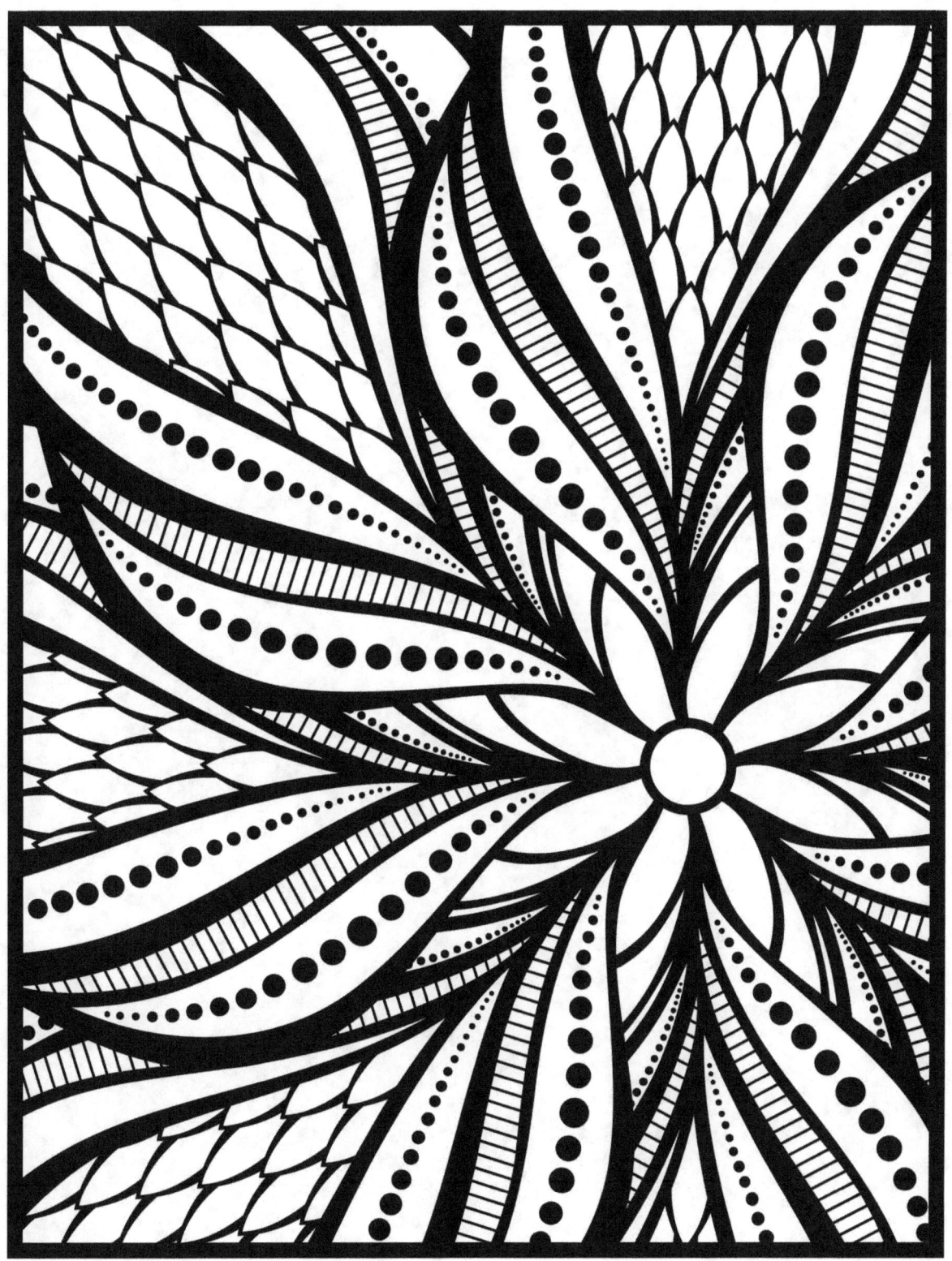

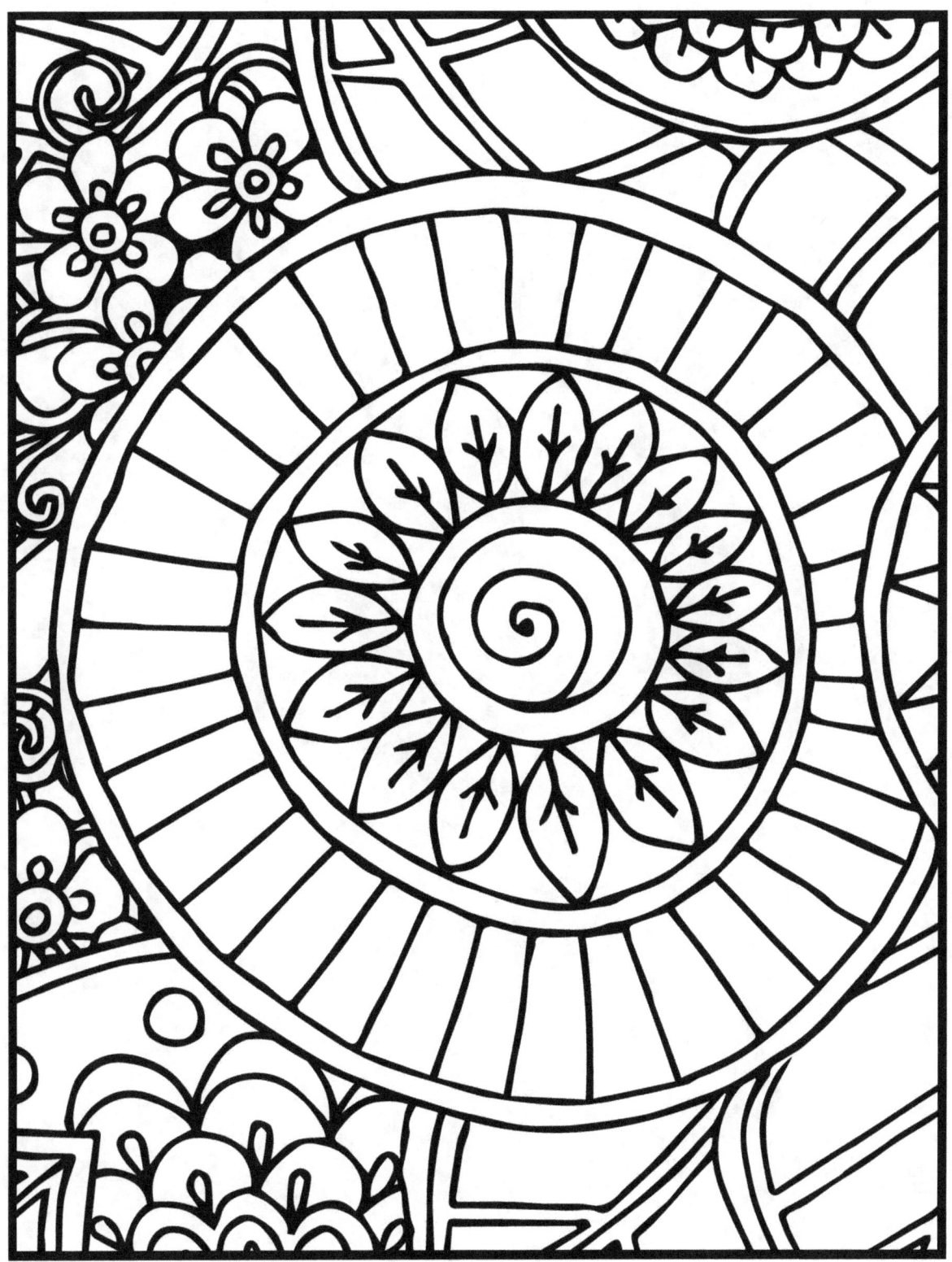

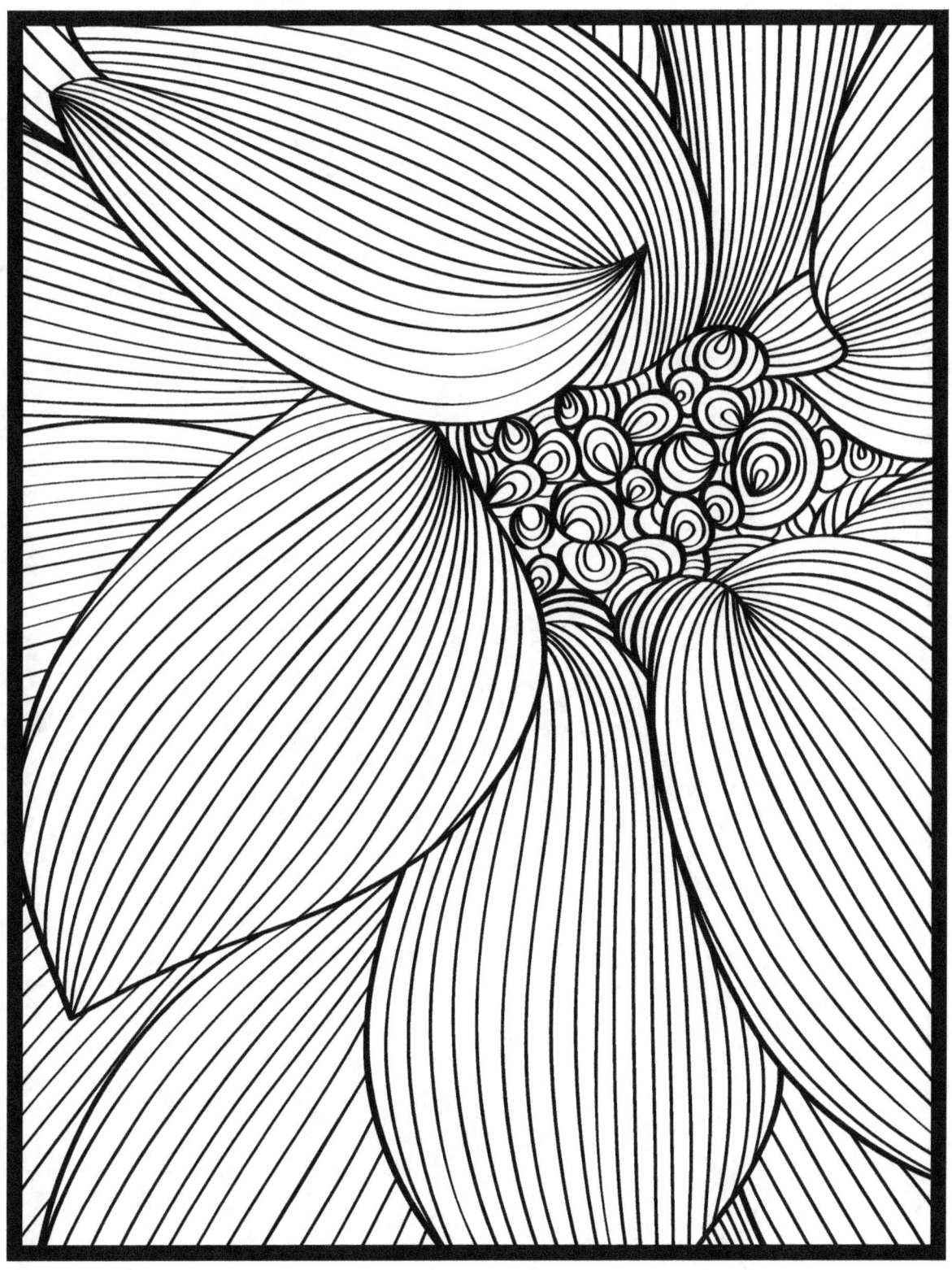

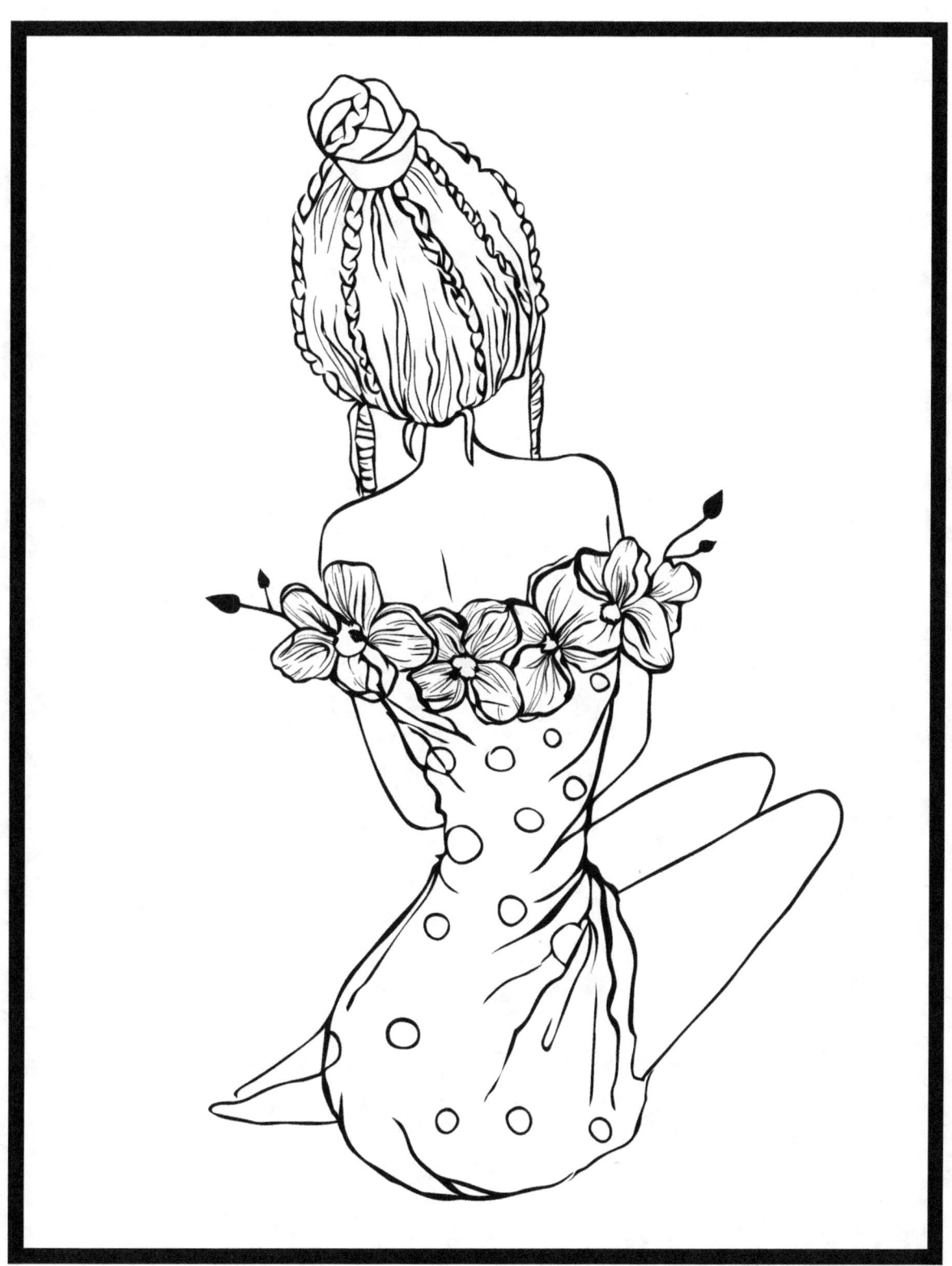

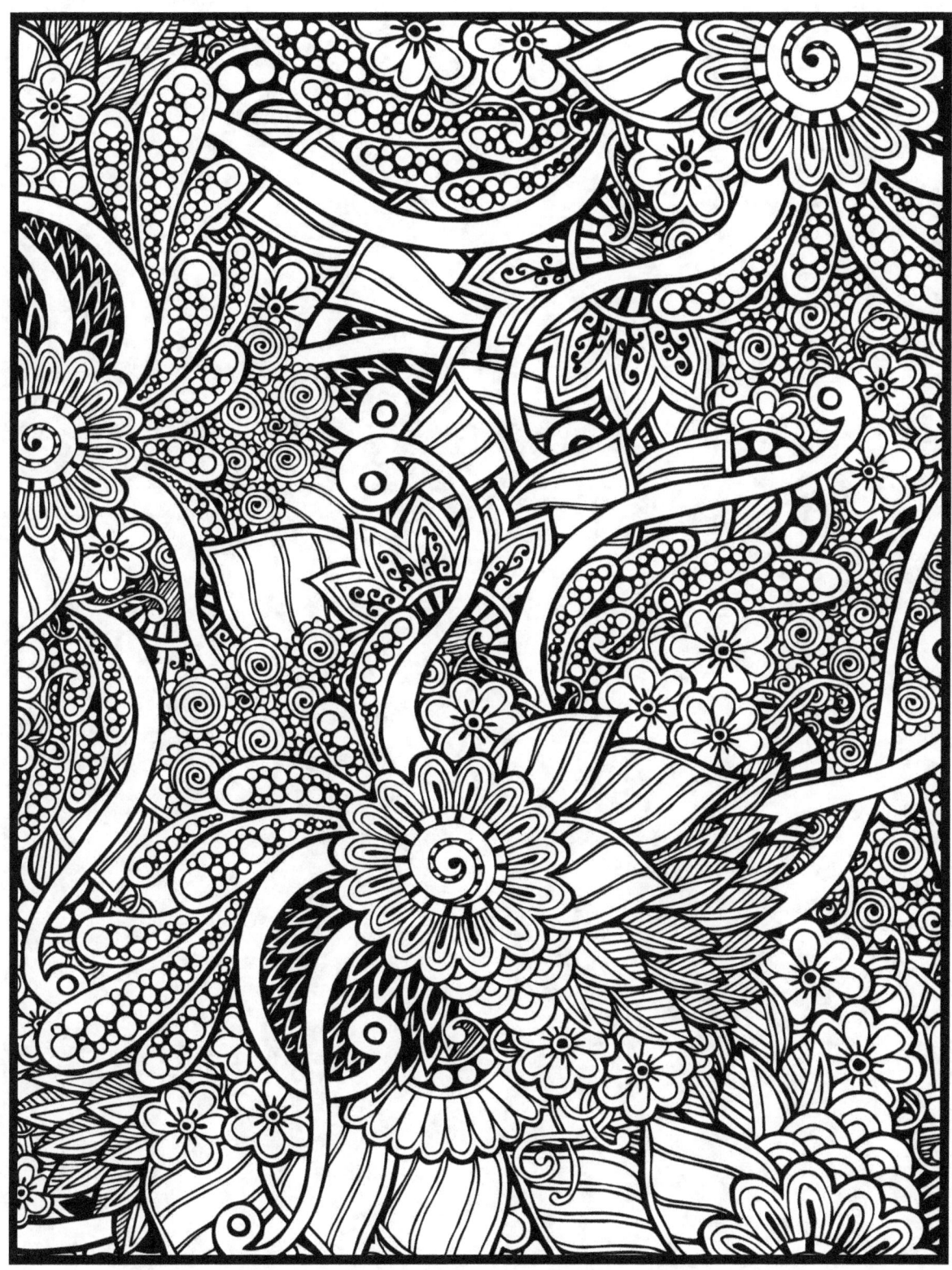

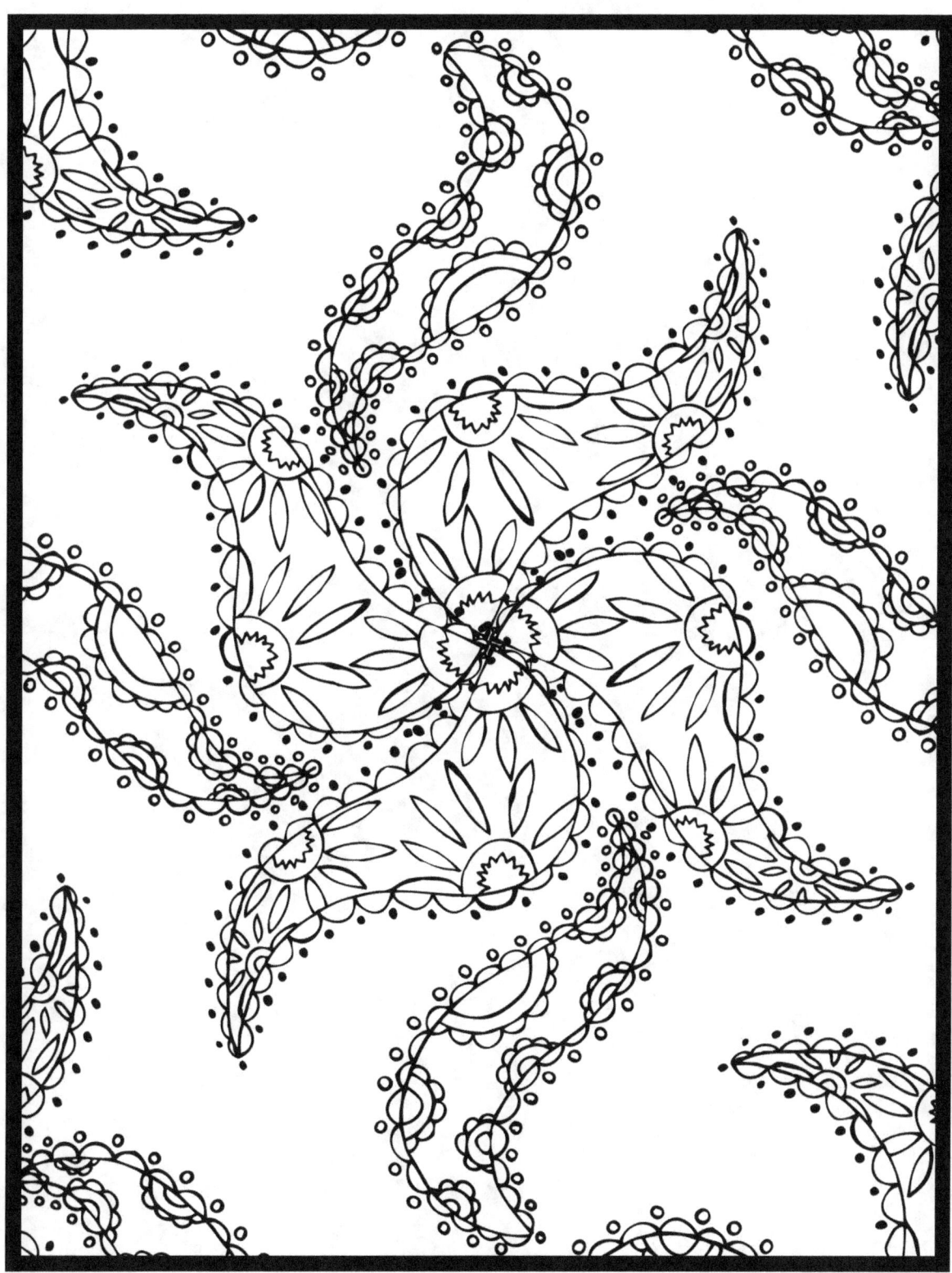

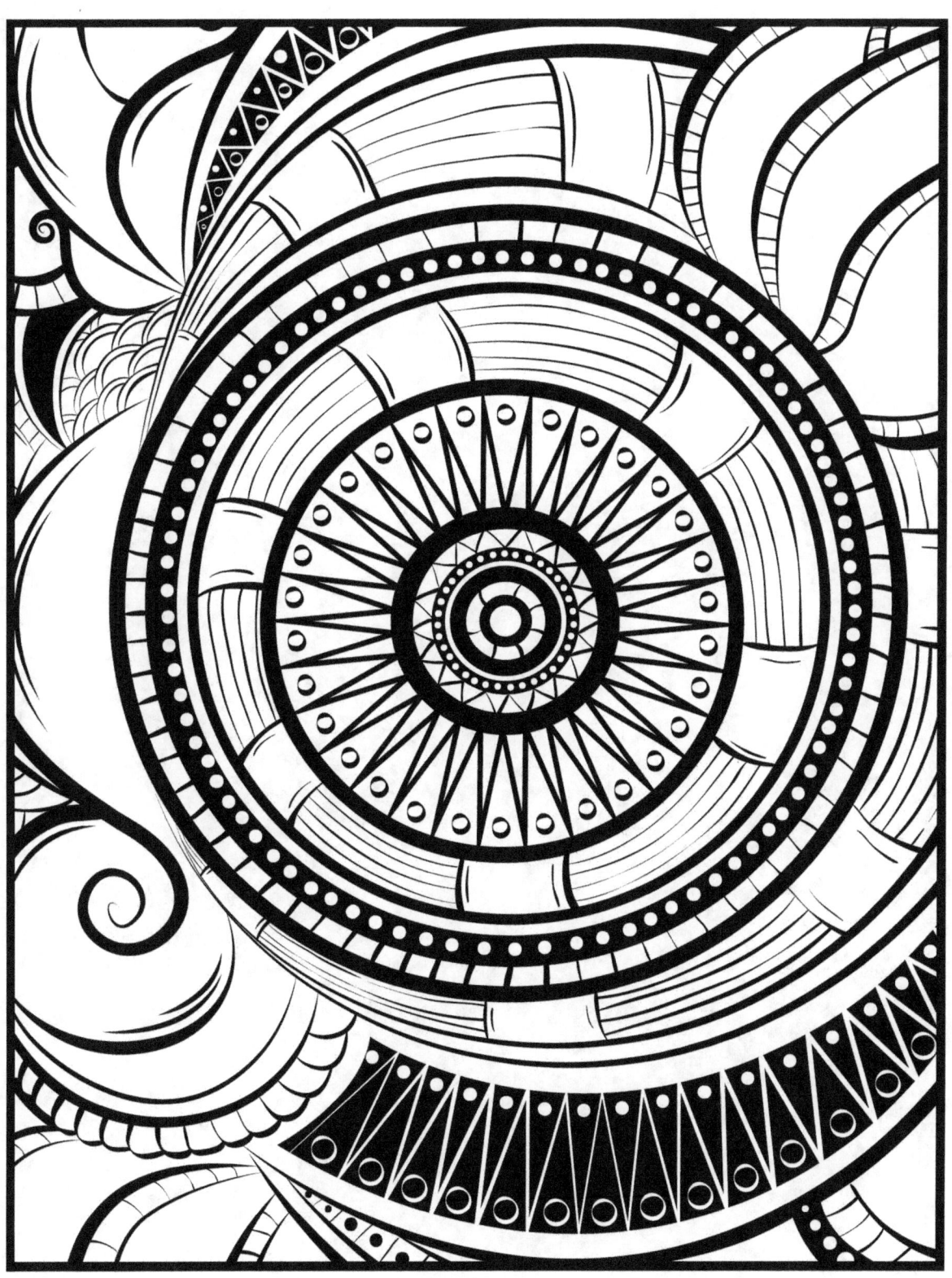

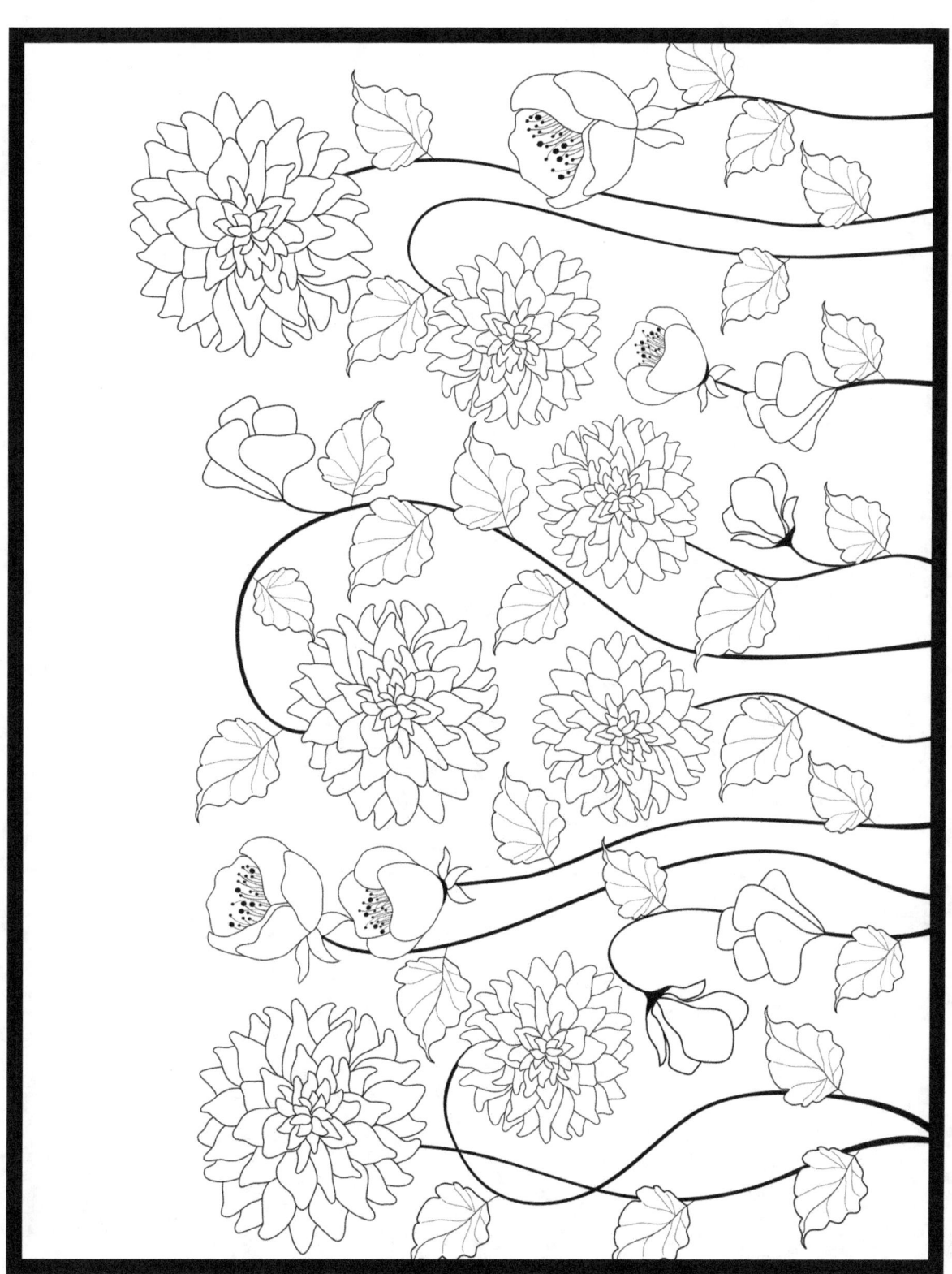

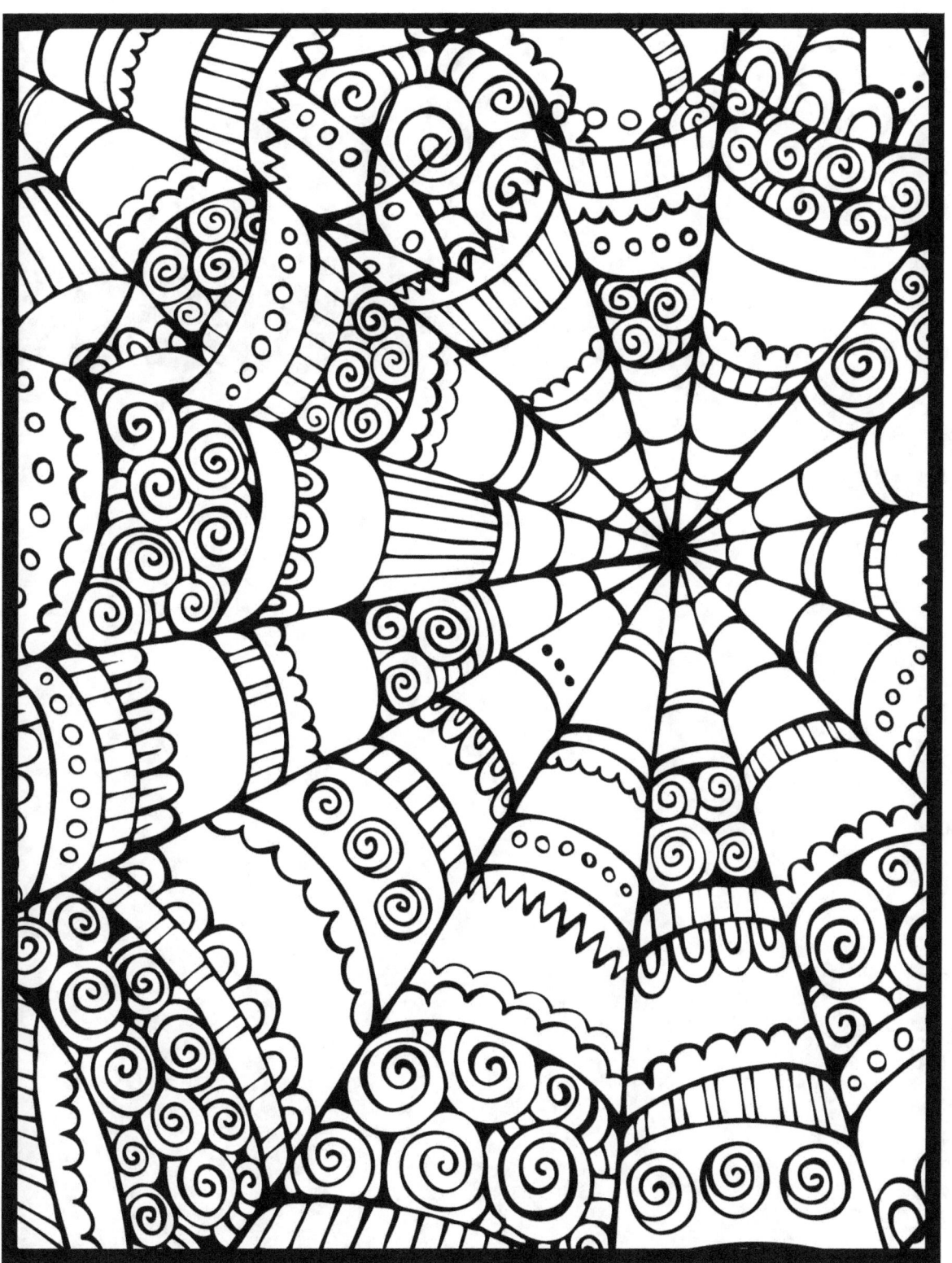

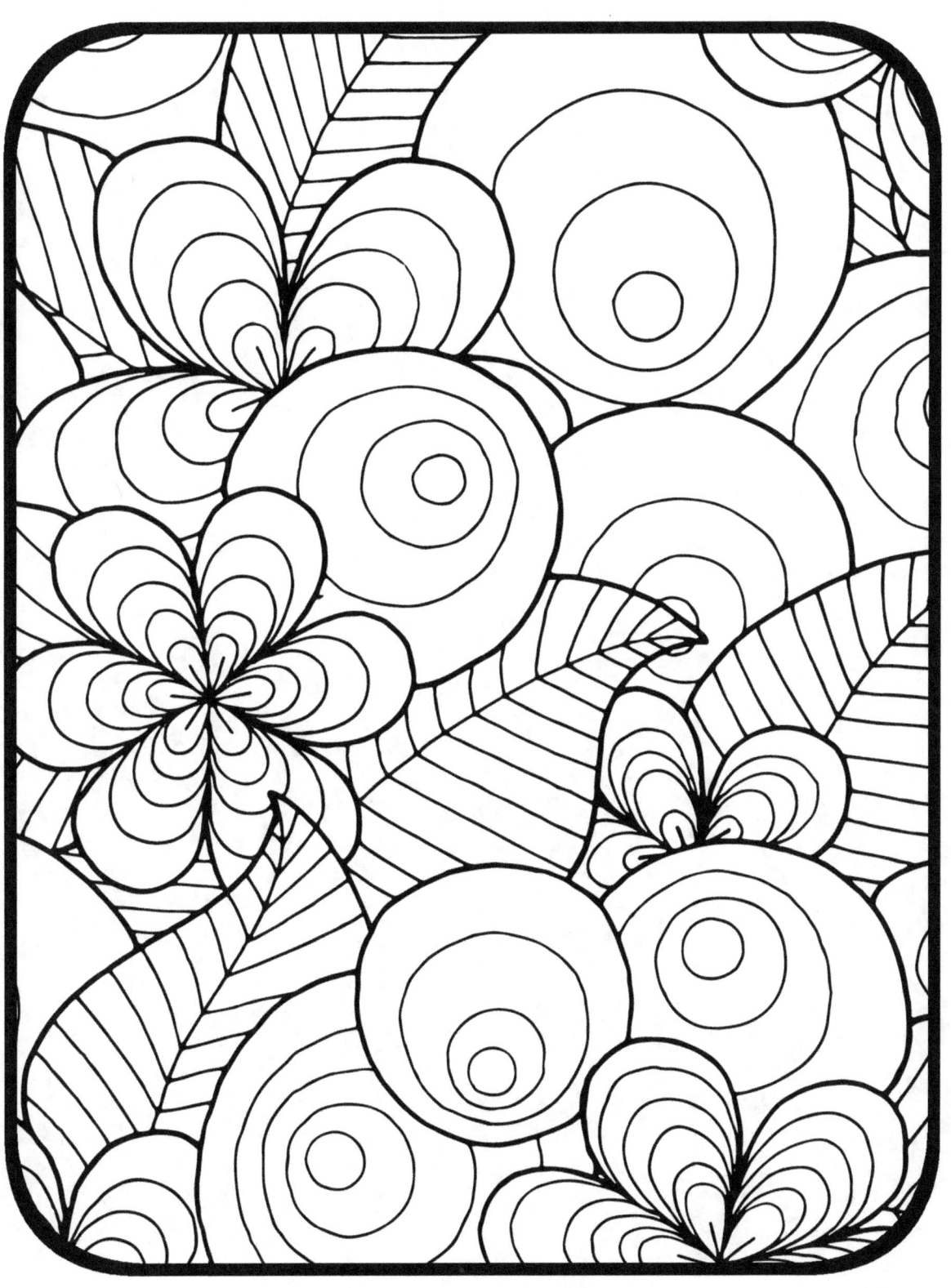

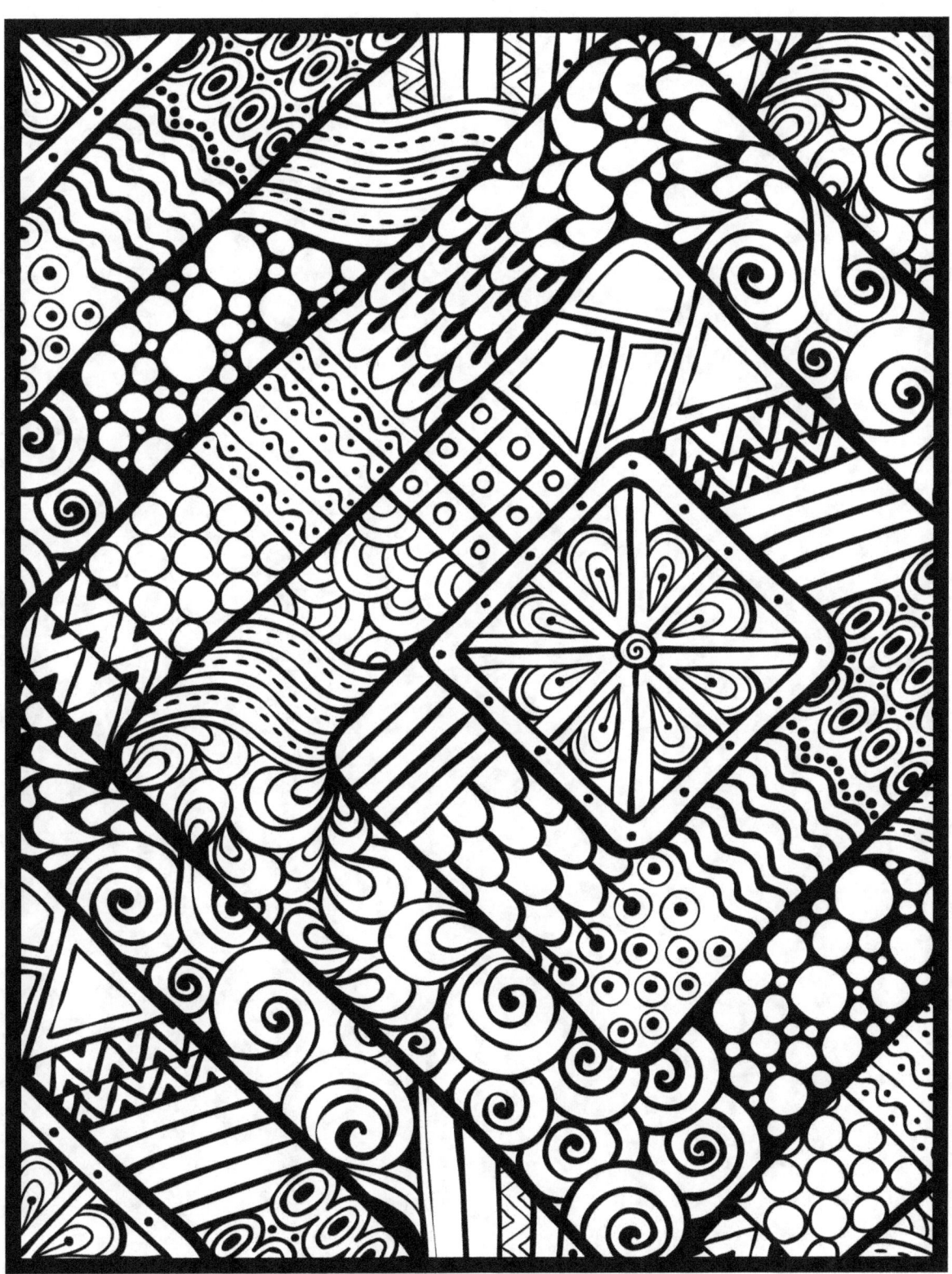

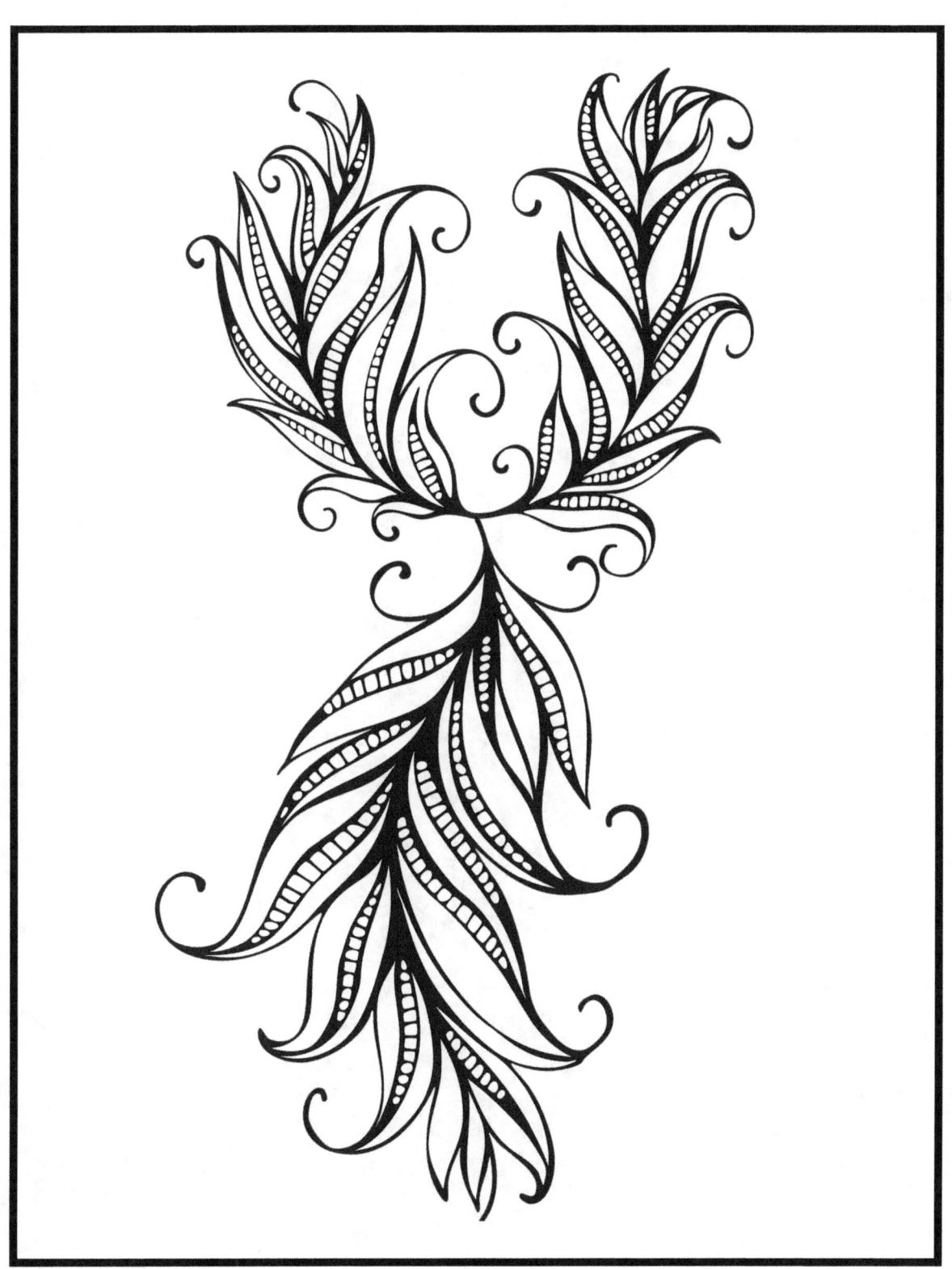

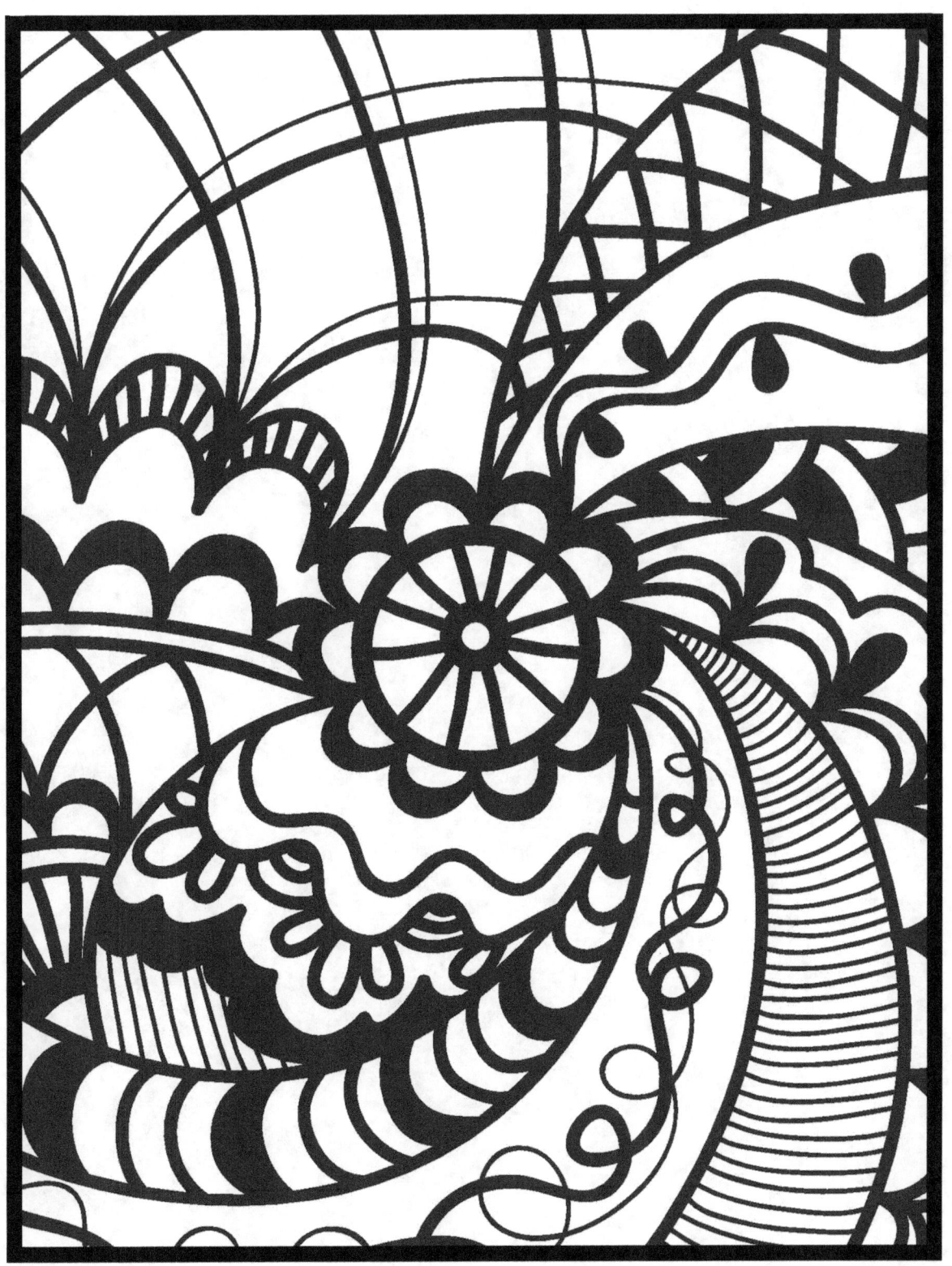

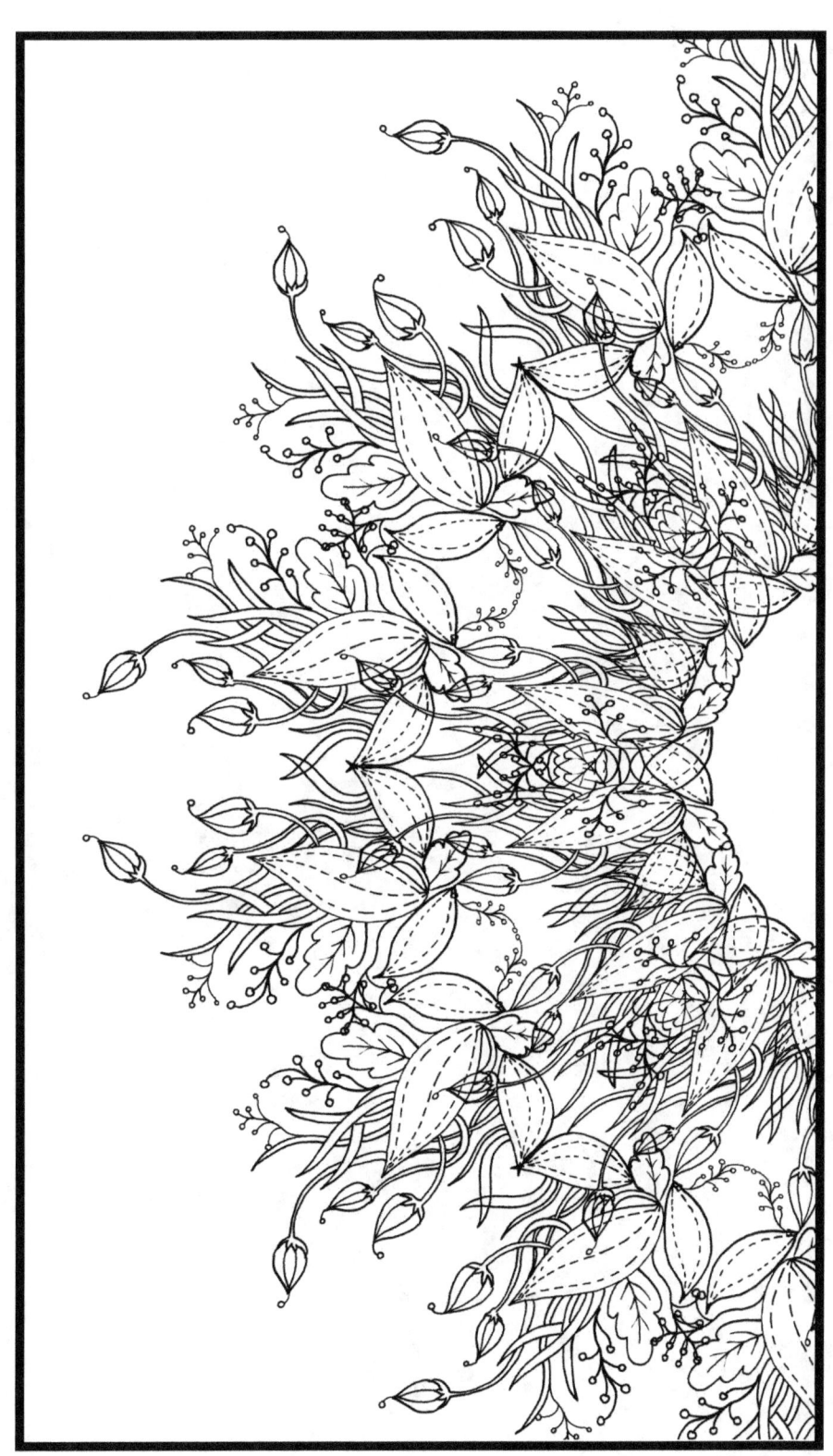

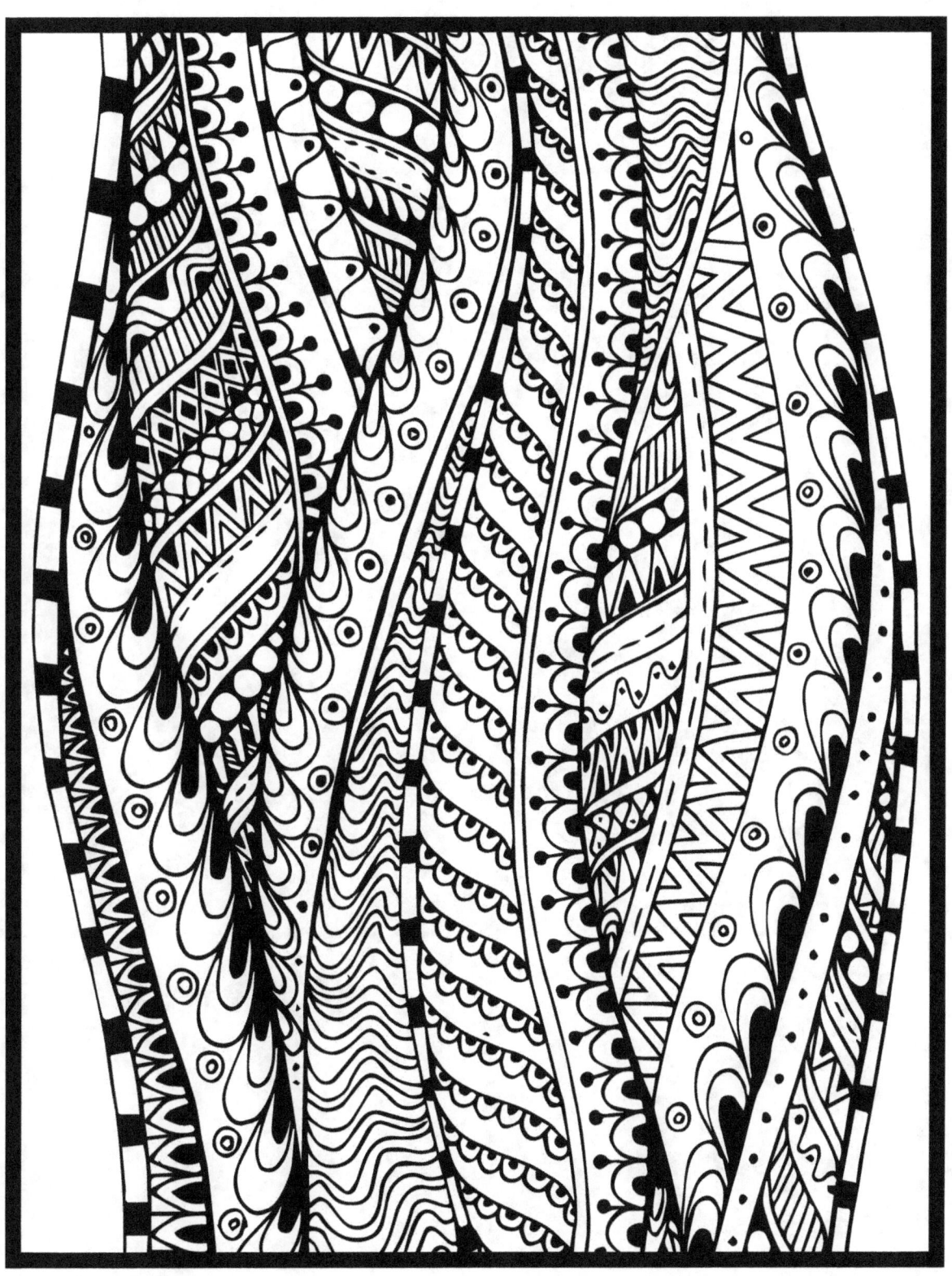

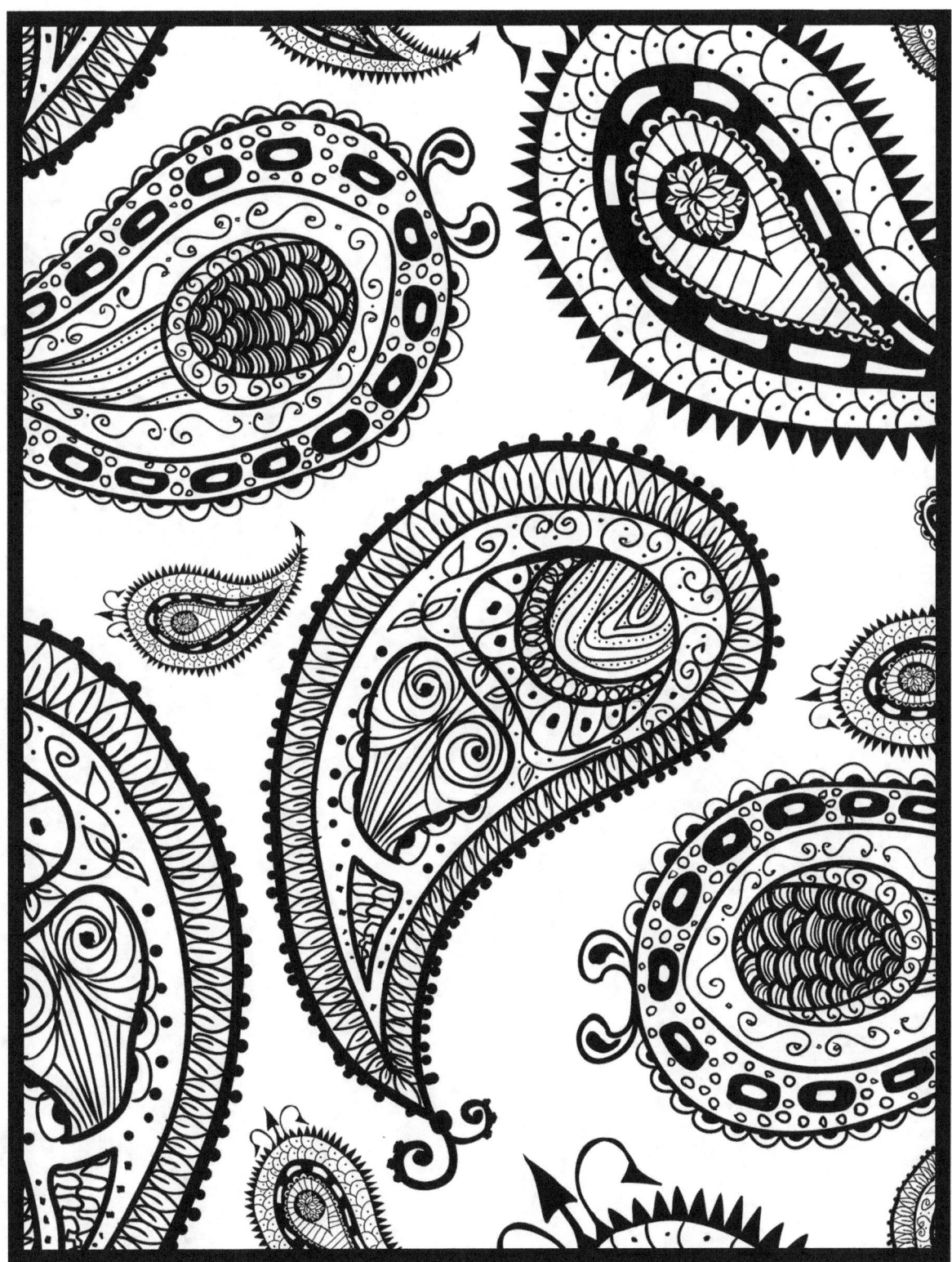

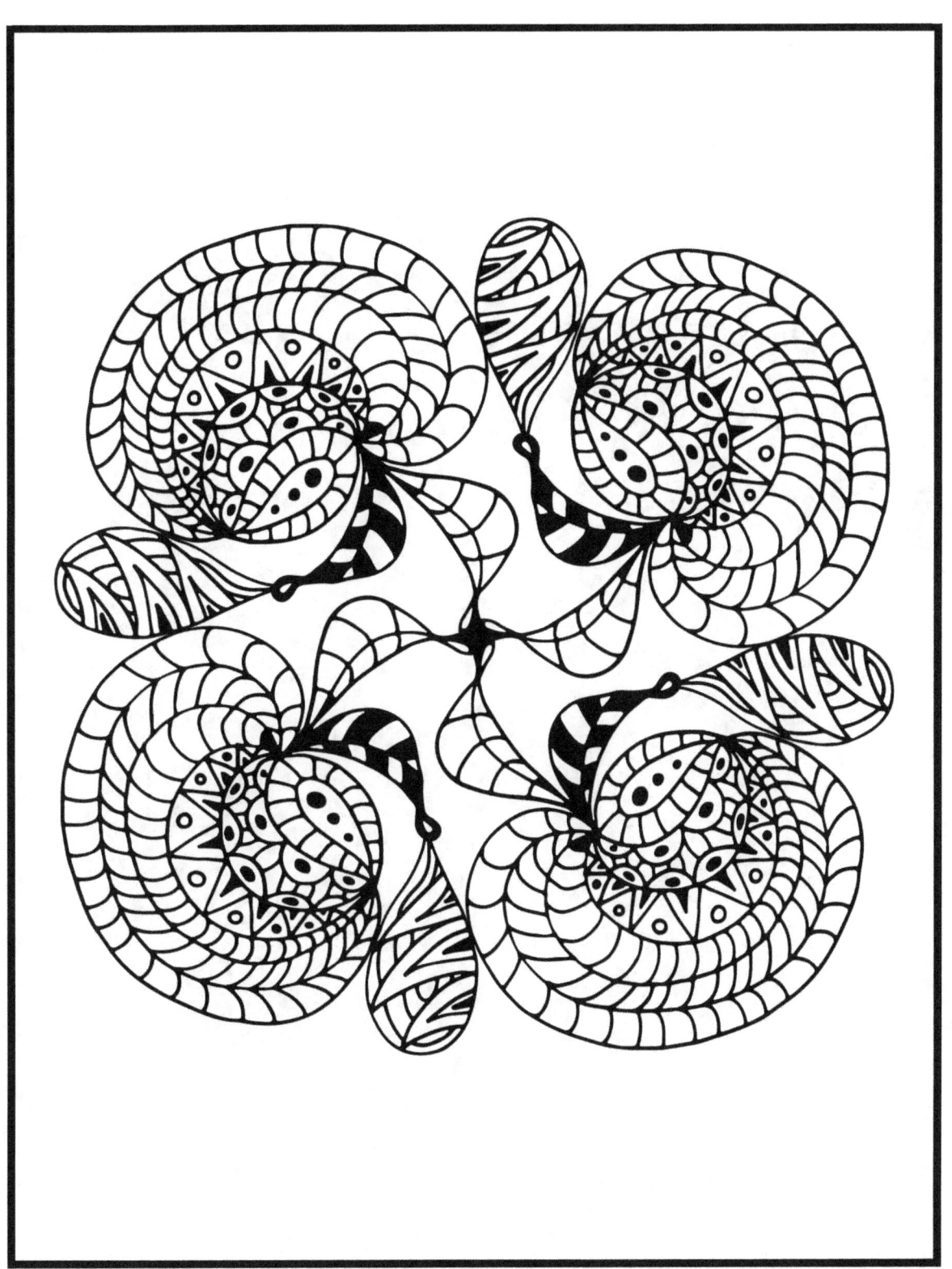

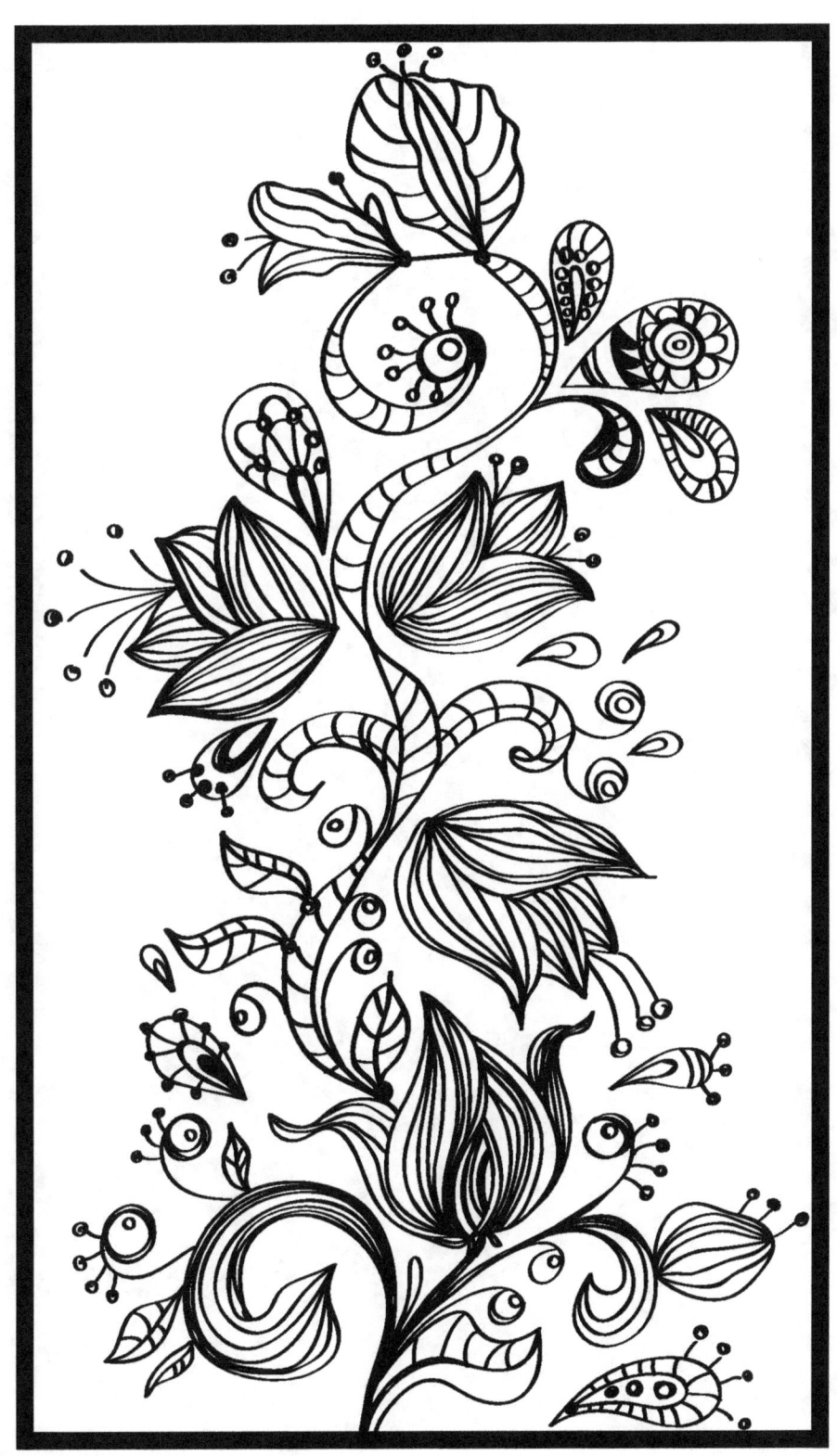

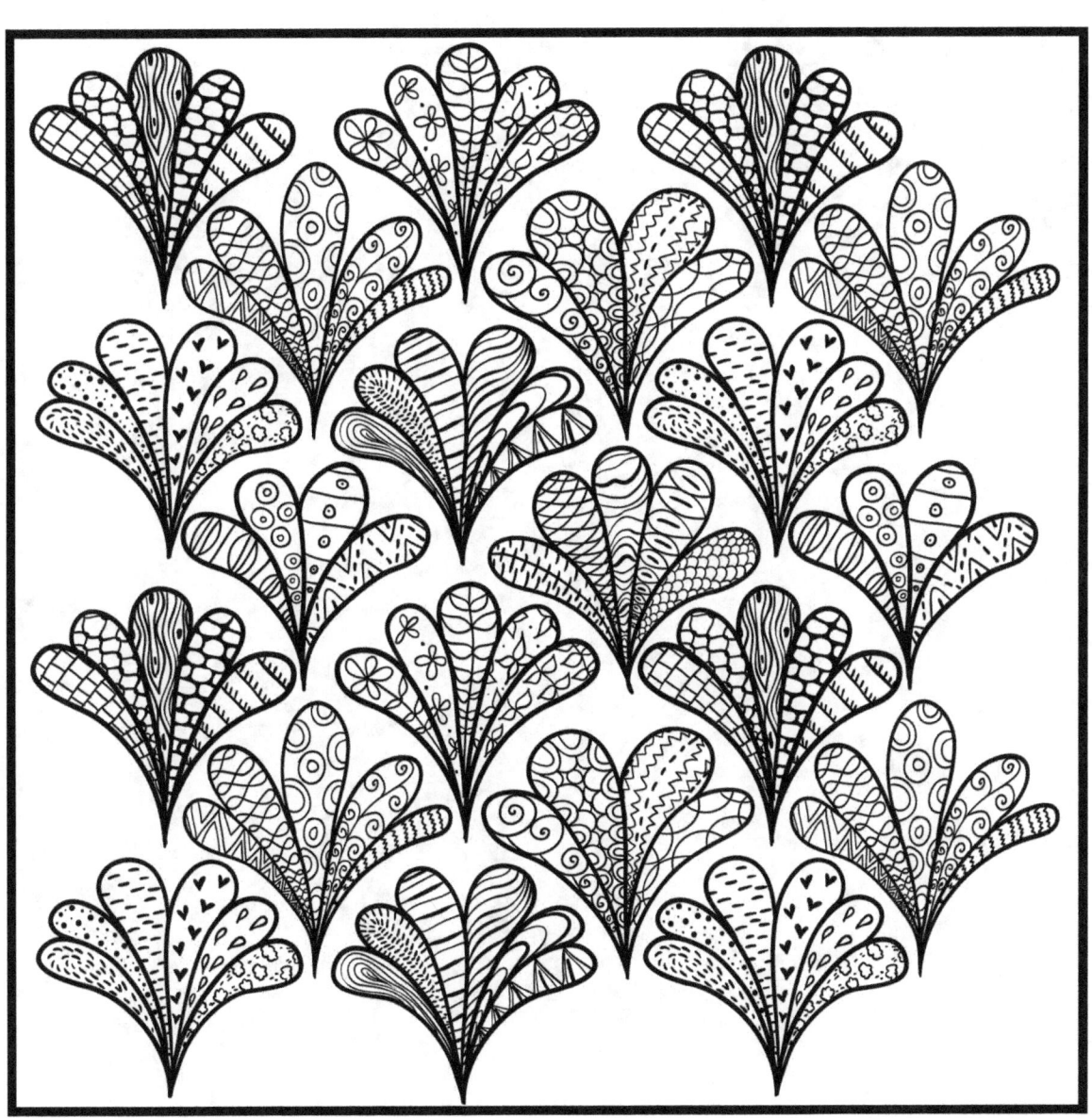

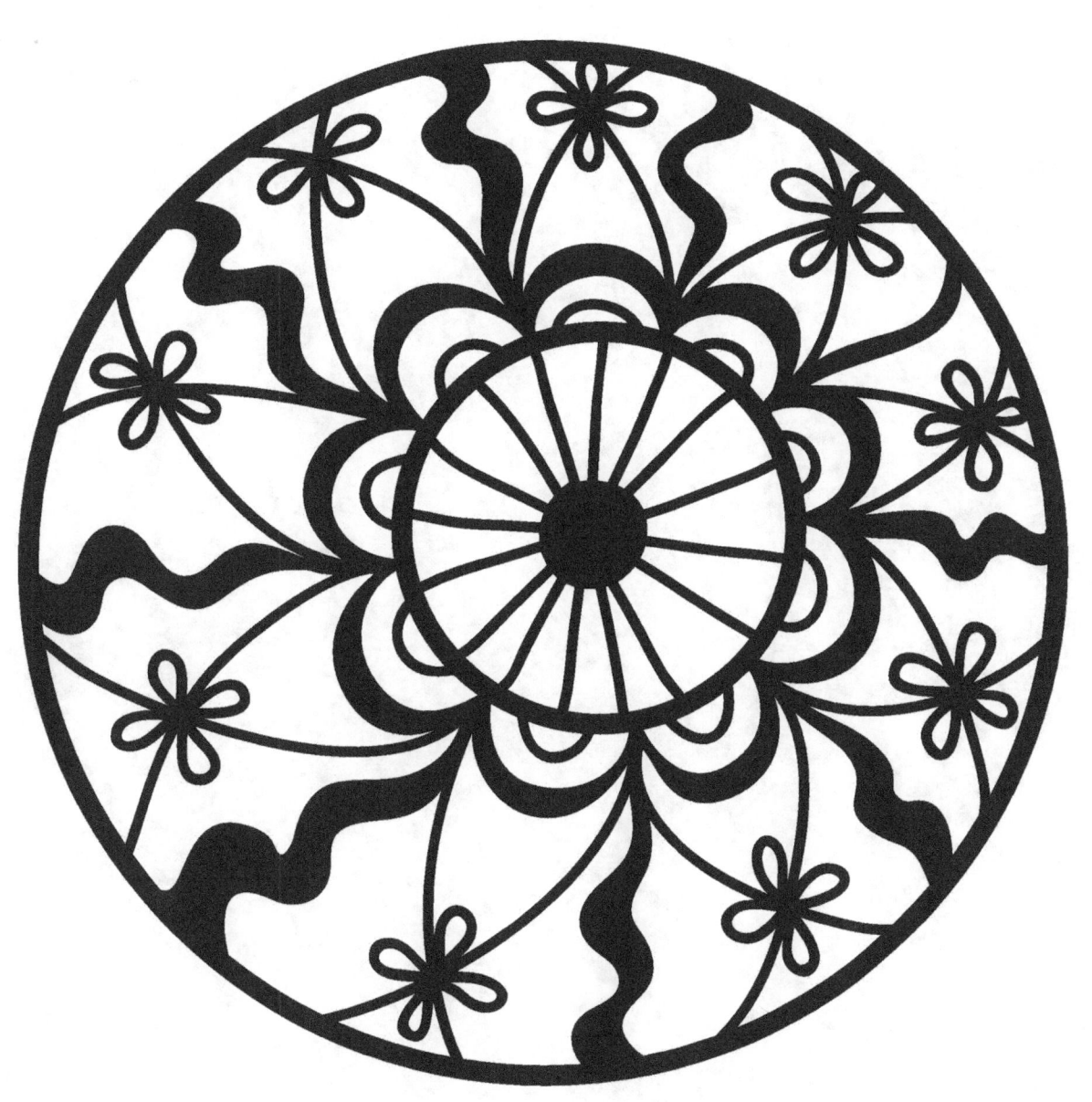

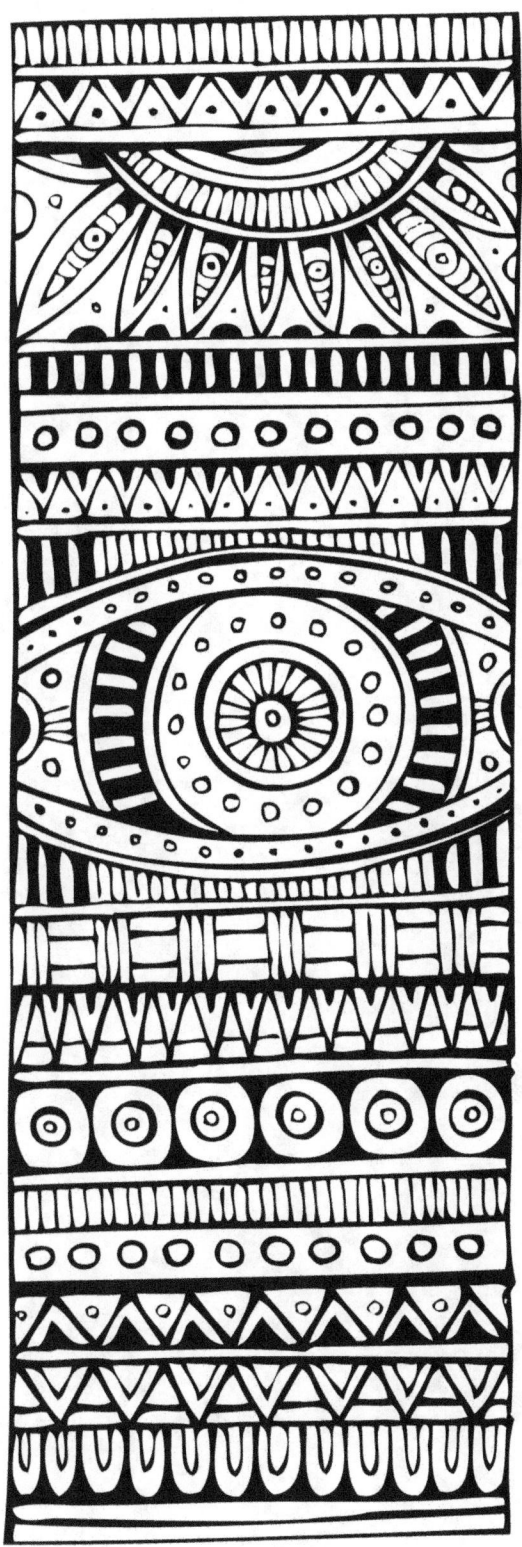
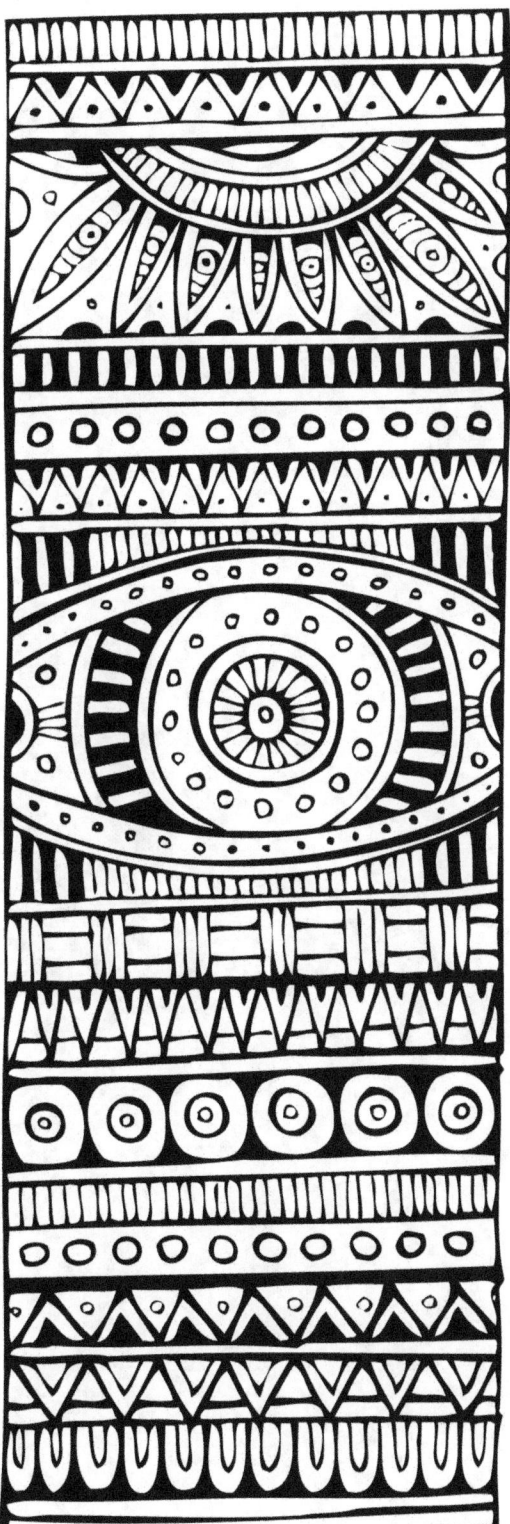

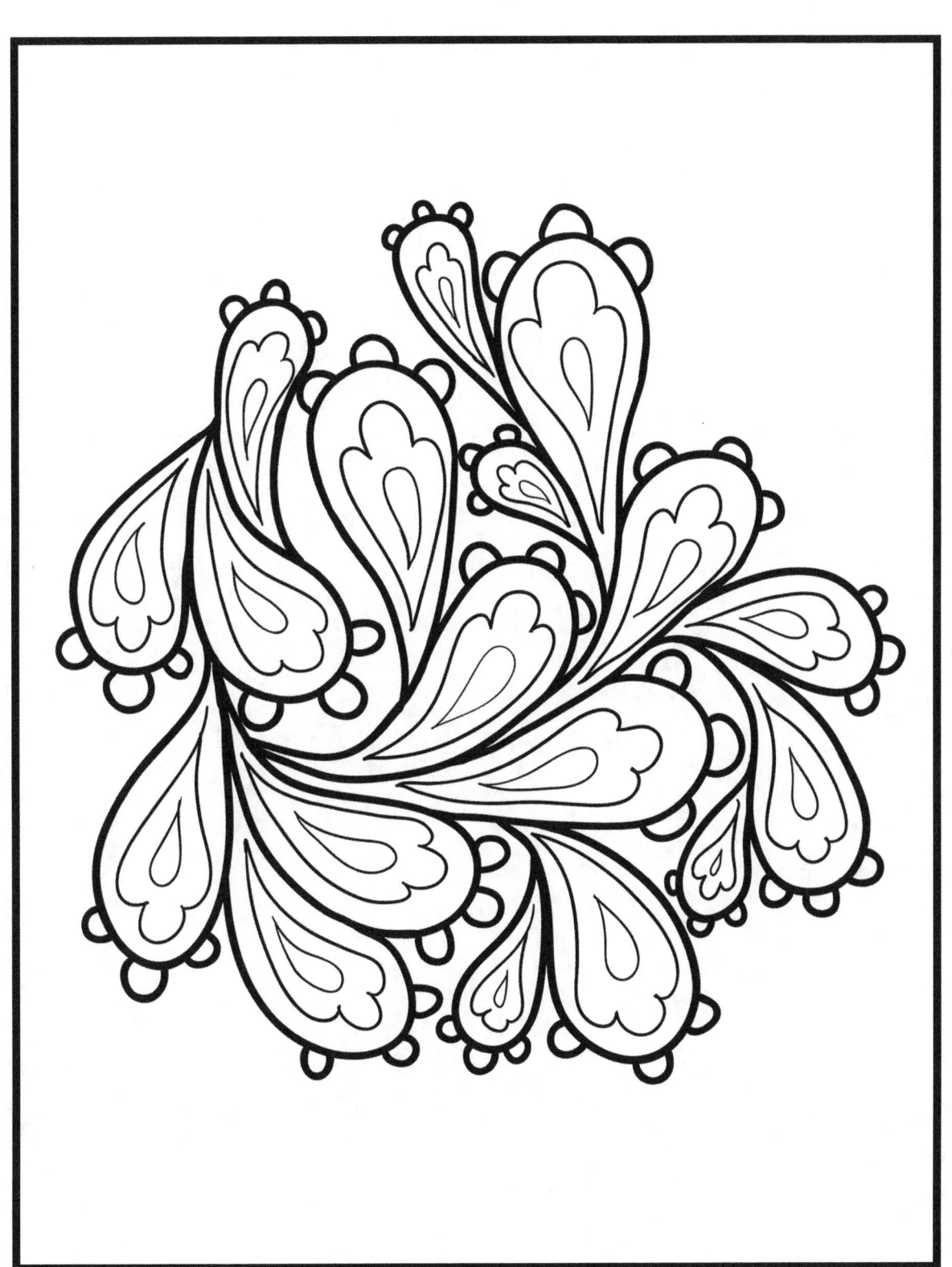

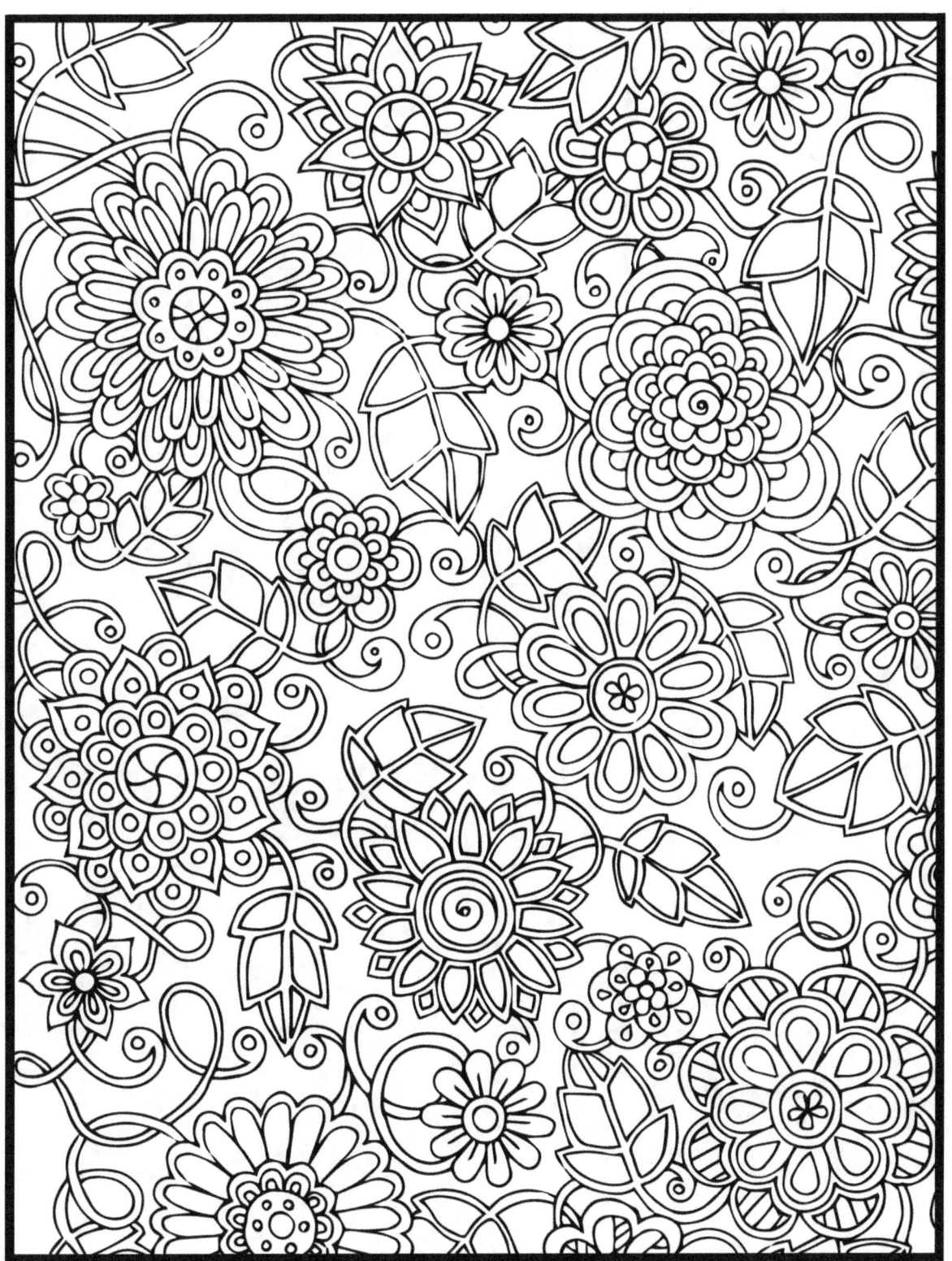

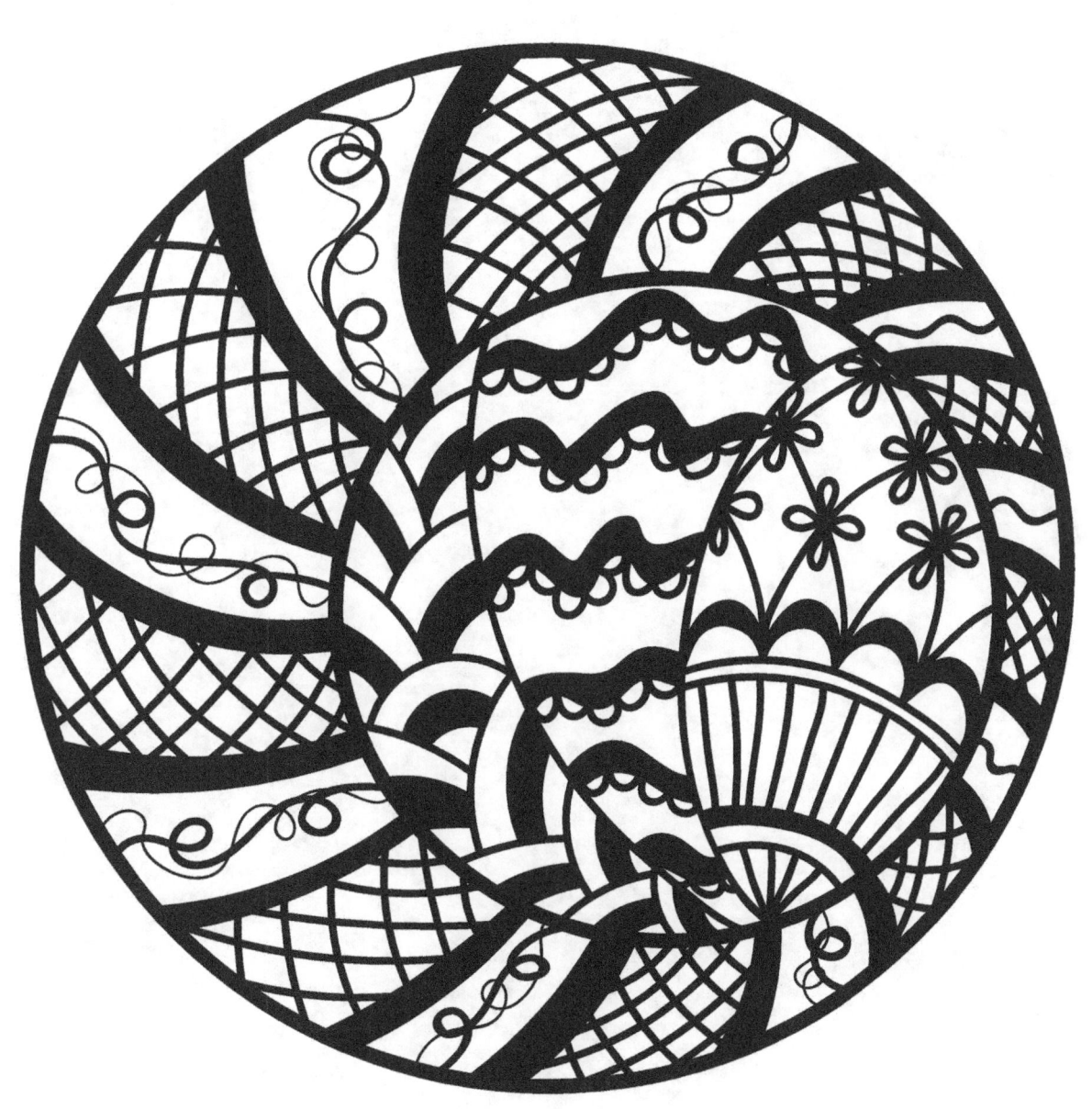

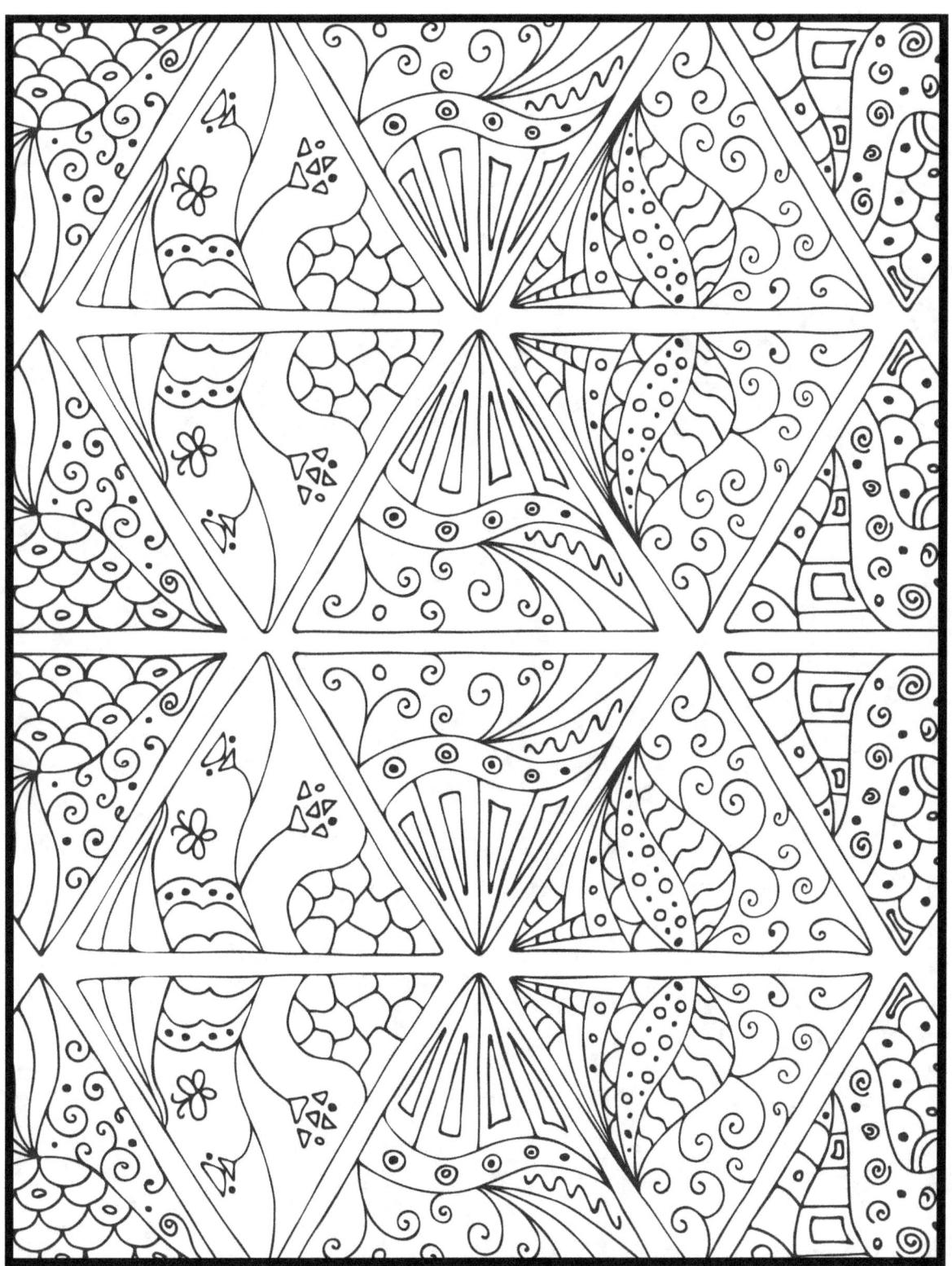

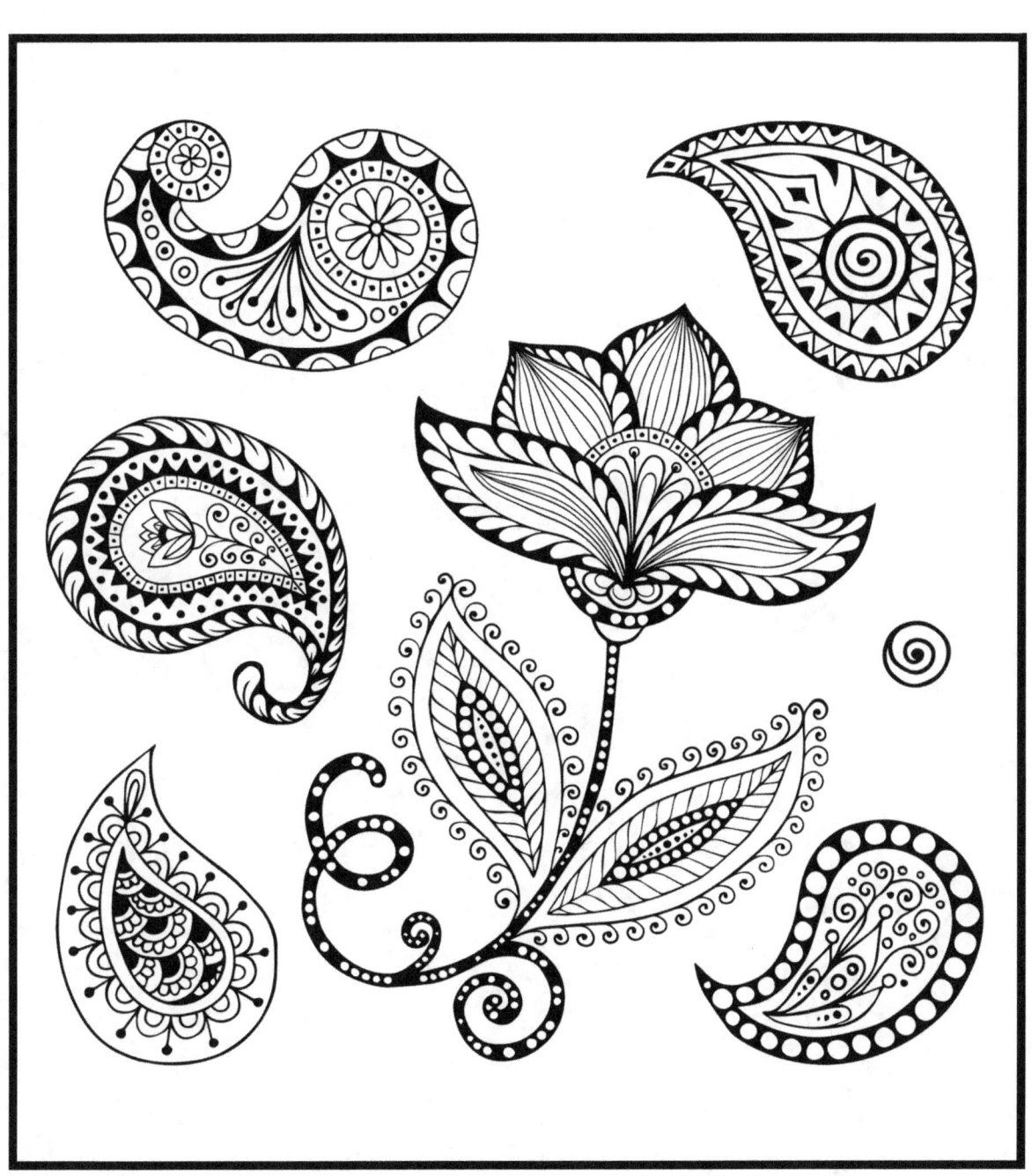

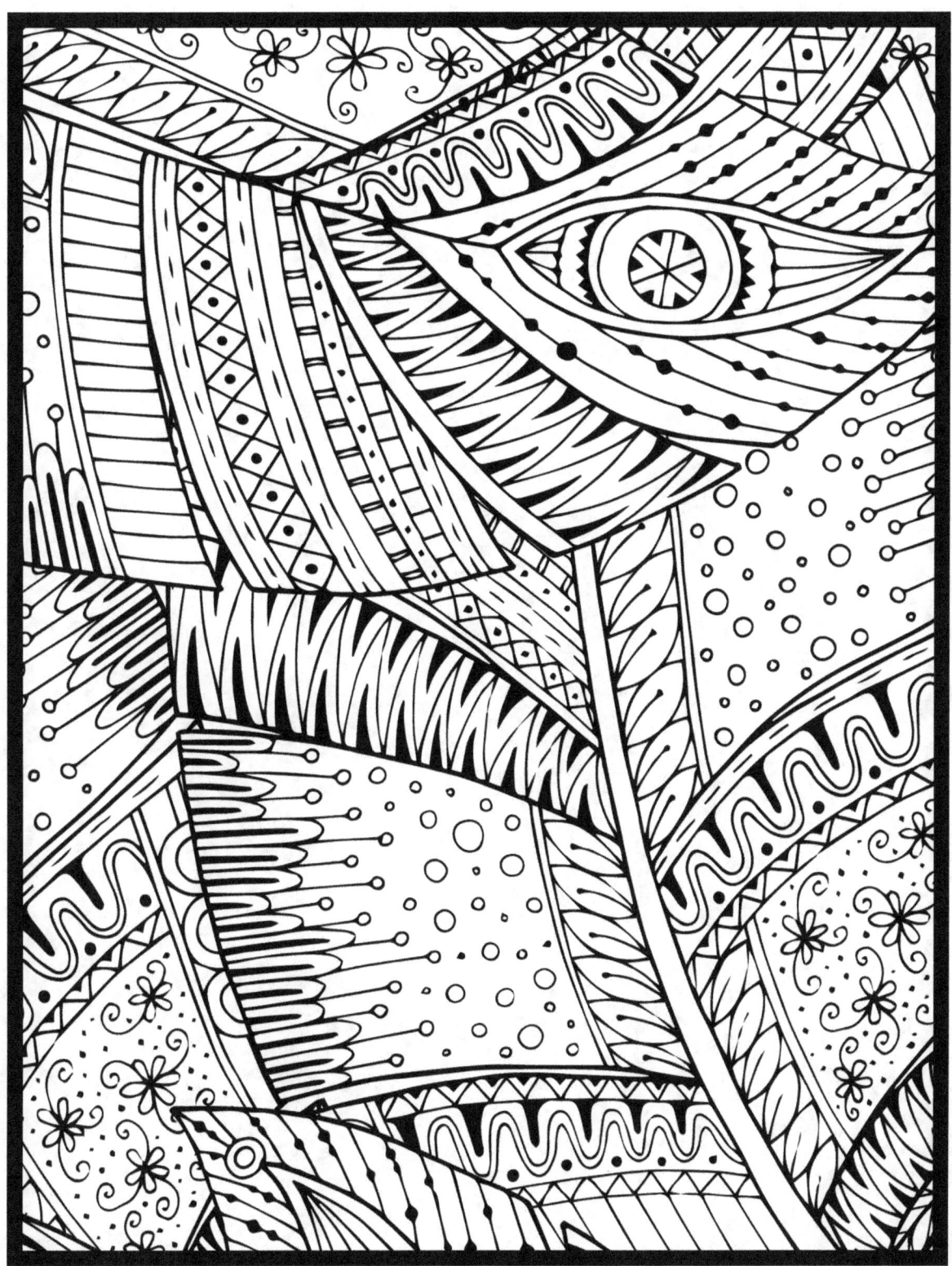

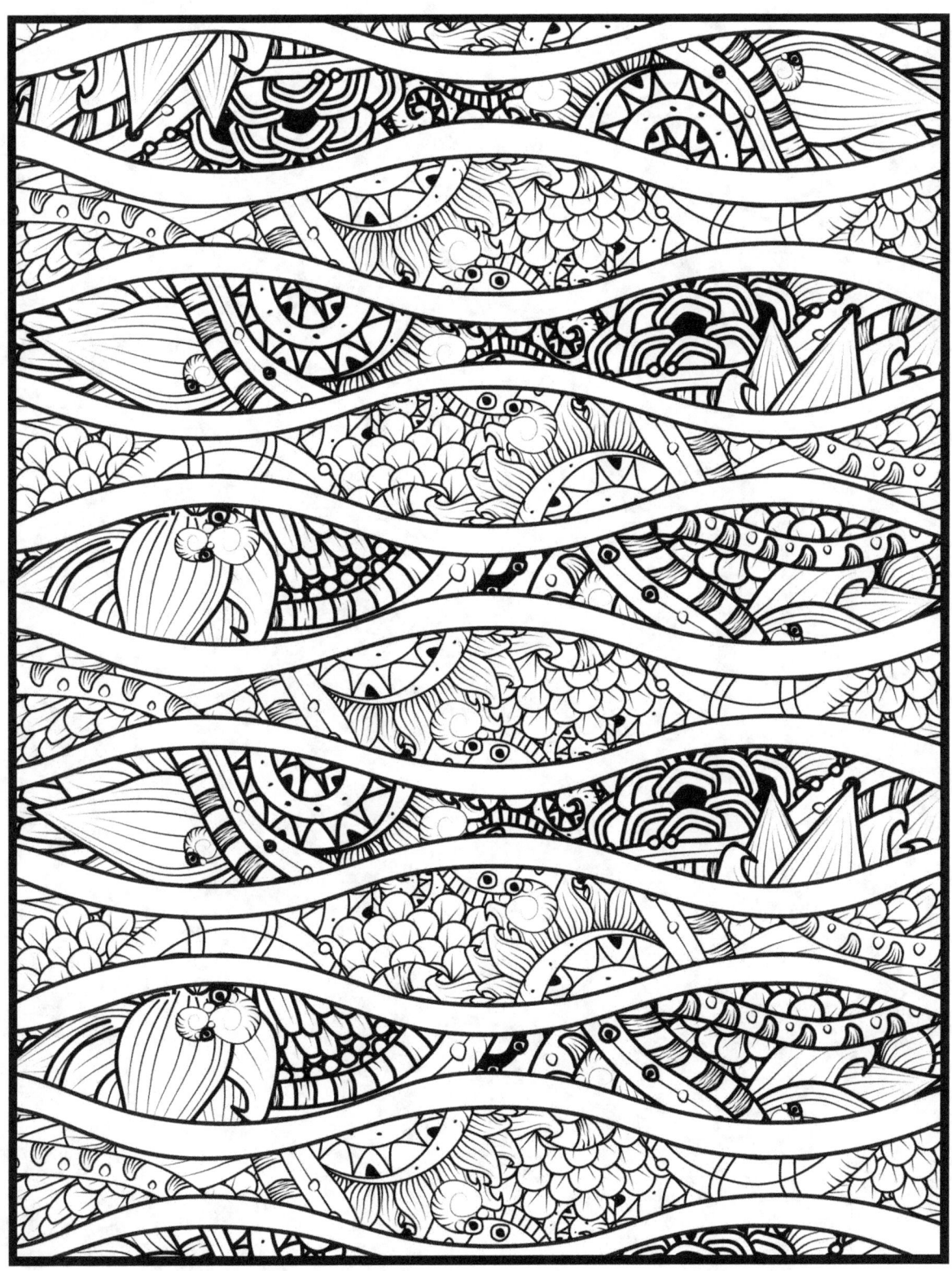

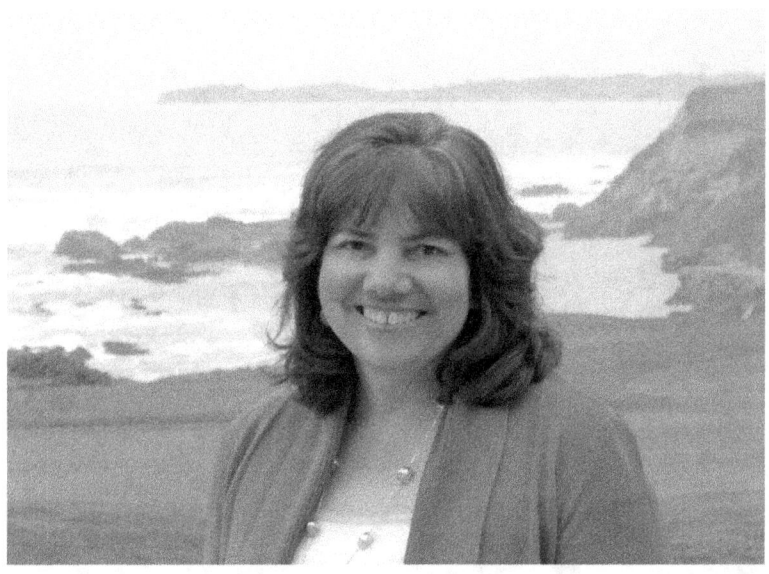

Barbara Freethy is a #1 New York Times Bestselling Author of 42 novels ranging from contemporary romance to romantic suspense and women's fiction. Traditionally published for many years, Barbara opened her own publishing company in 2011 and has since sold over 5 million copies of her books. Twenty of her titles have appeared on the New York Times and USA Today Bestseller Lists.

For more information, visit Barbara's website at www.barbarafreethy.com
Join her on Facebooks at www.facebook.com/barbarafreethybooks
Follow her on Twitter at www.twitter.com/barbarafreethy